Constellated Ministry

Contemporary and Historical Paganism

Series Editors

Chas S. Clifton, Colorado State University-Pueblo
Scott Simpson, Institute of European Studies, Jagiellonian University

This series seeks original work on contemporary and revived Pagan religious traditions around the world, as well as re-examinations of ancient polytheistic religion from new perspectives. Contributions are invited from diverse disciplines, including religious studies, popular culture, musicology, anthropology, sociology, ethnography, and feminist philosophy of religion.

Published

Being Viking
Heathenism in Contemporary America
Jefferson Calico

Forthcoming

Albion's Sage for the New Age
John Michell, Radical Traditionalism and the Myth of Sacred England
Marleen Thaler

The Spider Dance
Tradition, Time and Healing in Southern Italy
Giovanna Parmigiani

Constellated Ministry
A Guide for Those Serving Today's Pagans

Holli S. Emore

SHEFFIELD UK   BRISTOL CT

Published by Equinox Publishing Ltd

UK: Office 415, The Workstation, 15 Paternoster Row, Sheffield, South Yorkshire S1 2BX
USA: ISD, 70 Enterprise Drive, Bristol, CT 06010

www.equinoxpub.com

First published 2021

© Holli S. Emore 2021

All rights reserved. No part of this publication may be reproduced or transmitted in any form or by any means, electronic or mechanical, including photocopying, recording or any information storage or retrieval system, without prior permission in writing from the publishers.

British Library Cataloguing-in-Publication Data

A catalogue record for this book is available from the British Library.
ISBN-13 978 1 78179 956 7 (hardback)
978 1 78179 957 4 (paperback)
978 1 78179 958 1 (ePDF)
978 1 80050 121 8 (ePub)

Library of Congress Cataloging-in-Publication Data

Names: Emore, Holli S, author.
Title: Constellated ministry : a guide for those serving today's pagans / Holli S Emore.
Description: Bristol, CT : Equinox Publishing Ltd, 2021. | Series: Contemporary and historical paganism | Includes bibliographical references and index. | Summary: "This volume reviews the shifting landscape of current Pagan spirituality, the unique culture and needs which must be understood in order to engage with contemporary Pagans, and the implications for future leadership, including organizational models, training and educational needs"-- Provided by publisher.
Identifiers: LCCN 2021001609 (print) | LCCN 2021001610 (ebook) | ISBN 9781781799567 (hardback) | ISBN 9781781799574 (paperback) | ISBN 9781781799581 (epdf) | ISBN 9781800501218 (epub)
Subjects: LCSH: Neopaganism. | Pastoral theology.
Classification: LCC BP605.N46 E46 2021 (print) | LCC BP605.N46 (ebook) | DDC 299/.94--dc23
LC record available at https://lccn.loc.gov/2021001609
LC ebook record available at https://lccn.loc.gov/2021001610

Typeset by S.J.I. Services, New Delhi, India

Contents

Introduction	1
1 The Changing Landscape of Today's Spiritualities	9
2 Who Are Contemporary Pagans?	20
3 A New Ministry Model	33
4 Stories From Pagan Leaders	49
5 Moving Into The Future	70
6 Vision for the Future	117
Resources	120
Bibliography	123
Appendix: Group or Solitary: Choices and Spiritual Care Needs in Contemporary Pagan Practice	129
Index	173

Introduction

Why should Pagans be trained in the art of ministry? As this new religious movement matures, some readily embrace patterns of service which already exist in our society. Then there are some Pagans who declare they do not want anyone to minister to them. Being someone who is often called upon for spiritual support, I've often puzzled over this quandary.

Recently, I led a discussion group in comparing the Fisher King of Arthurian legend with Osiris of ancient Egypt. Each has suffered a mortal wound. The Fisher King lingers on, but his wound will not heal, and while he suffers the land suffers, too, the wasteland of T. S. Eliot's poem. Osiris dies, but he lives on as king of the afterworld realm. The cycle of the dry season was observed as the time he is inert in his grave. The Nile flood returns Osiris to potency with its life-giving waters and black silt, and the growing season is evidence that he is alive again in the land. Another part of the Osirian myth has his body being dismembered after his murder, then the parts reassembled by his devoted consort, Isis.

We do not know what compels some of us to gather the broken people, bind up their wounds, and nurse them back to health. We are told that some run away from a fire and others run towards it, to rescue. Each of these responses is acceptable, because not all of us are equipped to face either a fire, or those with wounds of the soul. *Constellated Ministry* is for the ones with a genuine desire to support Pagan spiritual needs.

Pagan traditions are the fastest-growing religious group in America, or so it has often been said since Wicca (British witchcraft) arrived on these shores in the late 1950s. Proto-Neopagan groups like the Church of Aphrodite predated even that wave of Wicca. Numbers are tricky to come by, but we know that contemporary Pagans report themselves as living in every American state and in countries around the world. Historian Ronald Hutton is fond of pointing out that modern Pagan witchcraft is the one new religion that England has produced and shared globally.[1]

Naturally, many of these individuals have come together to form covens, kindreds, hearths, circles, and goddess groups, as well as prison ministries, educational institutions, clergy training programs, and more. Pagans volunteer for community projects like food banks and animal shelters, work in regional interfaith groups, and have provided valuable national and international leadership for organizations such as the Parliament of the World's Religions, the United Religions Initiative, and the North American Interfaith Network.

But the Pagan Engagement and Spiritual Support survey of 2017 showed that a large majority of Pagans continue to practice their spirituality alone, as "solitaries." Those findings were consistent with research of

---

1 Ronald Hutton, *The Triumph of the Moon: A History of Modern Pagan Witchcraft* (Oxford: Oxford University Press, 1999), vi.

past years by Helen Berger[2] and Gwendolyn Reece.[3] By stark contrast, scholars like Robert Putnam, Robert Bellah, and Robert Wuthnow have drawn attention to the ways that declining social ties have weakened society. This comes at a time when many Americans and people in other Western countries report their religious identity as "spiritual but not religious," or "SBNR."[4] These are also often called "nones" because in surveys they have marked their religion as "none," or unaffiliated. In fact, nearly 74 percent of those responding to my own Pagan Engagement and Spiritual Support survey, which I conducted in 2017, described themselves as either spiritual or SBNR, and only 16 percent considered themselves "religious."[5]

If "solitary" has described most Pagans for well over a decade, then what about the mushrooming of covens and other groups which appeared in the 1980s and 1990s? Sometimes compared to the house church movement of the 1970s, or the small groups movement within churches in the 1990s and 2000s, the stereotypical witches' or Druid circle of a dozen or so members looks like the ideal structure for a new religious movement. Indeed, as far as we know, many religions around the world have probably started in this manner.

2   Berger, Helen A., Evan A. Leach, and Leish S. Shaffer, *Voices from the Pagan Census: A National Survey of Witches and Neo-pagans in the United States* (Columbia: University of South Carolina, 2013), 118.
3   Reece, Gwendolyn, "Prevalence and Importance of Contemporary Pagan Practices," *The Pomegranate: The International Journal of Pagan Studies* 16, no. 1 (2014): 12.
4   Linda A. Mercadante, *Belief without Borders: Inside the Minds of the Spiritual but Not Religious* (Oxford: Oxford University Press, 2014).
5   Holli S. Emore, "Group or Solitary: Choices and Spiritual Care Needs in Contemporary Pagan Practice," Cherry Hill Seminary (Columbia, South Carolina, 2018).

Unfortunately, given the still-nascent stage of contemporary Paganism's growth, it is unlikely that the near future will bring a surge of available options for those who are unable to access a local group. No doubt many will still prefer autonomy, seeking spiritual support only when it is occasionally needed. Still others will experience some degree of isolation due to the somewhat nomadic modern existence driven by work and personal relocations.

In our time, the drive to achieve personal fulfillment has led to a kind of hyper-individualism. Our desire to be free agents of our own destiny has provoked great waves of creativity—the Renaissance, the Age of Reason, the Industrial Revolution, and even the countless self-help movements of the twentieth century. Individualism brings with it, however, a burden of responsibility to balance self-interest and social commitment. The benefits of group affiliation on health and mental health are widely accepted by the general public. And yet it is possible, even likely, that we are witnessing the end of the age of religious institutions, arguably the most common center of social cohesion in America for at least two centuries. European societies of the past also featured religious foci, particularly in small village life, until the growth of secularism of the past century precipitated a steady decline of religiosity in many areas. With such uncertainty, those who feel compelled to build community and offer spiritual support must find a way to offer their gifts in a way that respects the desires of group members and the boundaries of intentional solitaries.

Reconfiguring the Shape of Ministry

Many of us enjoyed stargazing as children, eagerly poring over maps of constellations and reading the myths of each figure outlined in the stars. Less well-known are other ancient maps of the same stars, telling the stories of other cultures, from ancient Egypt, Persia, and India. The endless possible constellations formed from the same fields of stars become a metaphor used here to discuss possibilities for a new vision of spiritual support and ministry that I call *constellated ministry*. Each star is a point of contact and potential interaction between a minister and those seeking guidance or support. Changing contexts will result in different constellations, different stories and varying as well as multiple approaches.

This volume reviews, at least briefly, the shifting landscape of current Pagan spirituality in America, the unique culture and needs which must be understood in order to engage with contemporary Pagans, and the implications for future leadership, including organizational models, training and educational needs. In addition to the Pagan Engagement survey, Pagan leaders around the U.S. agreed to be interviewed about their own experiences. As a practicing Pagan myself, I must disclose my own biases, but would like to think that my history lends depth to my understanding of the subject. Finally, having served as the executive director of a Pagan institution for more than a decade (Cherry Hill Seminary), I have lived daily with the questions prompting my studies and writing. For years, Pagan individuals and groups have contacted me for information and program advisement. In so doing, they have given me an invaluable window on the world of Pagan spirituality and spiritual needs. During these encounters, the same questions arose over and over again:

> What does "ministry" mean for Pagans?
> Whom do Pagans turn to for spiritual support?
> Who ought to be providing that support?
> Do Pagans want leaders who are trained for ministry?
> What kind of training do they need, and how do they get it?

Even while managing the day-to-day work of the seminary, doing what I could to inspire vision in our leadership, faculty, and students, I wondered how we could bridge what seemed like a gaping chasm between the worlds of traditional spiritual support (like so-called pulpit ministers, chaplains, rabbis, imams, and other leaders) and the organic, organizationally flat culture of Paganism. My years of nonprofit work and grant-writing haunted me, causing me to ask, just what are best practices for Pagan ministry or spiritual support? I kept coming back to the seeming co-occurrence of the rise of nones and SBNRs at the same time that most Pagans called themselves solitary. No previous research had done a deep dive into just why so many people were on their own. Was it because they could not access a group? Was it a personal choice? And, if the latter, then what did they do when they needed a spiritual hand, so to speak?

The stars merely glittered at me for a long time, holding their secrets close. Then I became involved in interfaith work, which in some ways resembles the wide and colorful umbrella of various traditions that scholars call Paganism. It took several years of regional and local interfaith activity before the celestial vault began to reflect for me a model of connecting Pagans in ways that could mirror both interdependence and individual authenticity. My various and diverse interfaith partners provided a living laboratory for observing the many ways that humans live their spirituality, both alone and with each other. To those partners I here offer heartfelt thanks. Meanwhile, my own Pagan group, Temple Osireion, matured and faithfully reflected with me as I made this journey of discovery.

Who Should Read This Book?

It's true that Pagans are largely non-institutional, with no paid ministers, and one rarely finds any kind of infrastructure to support what we normally think of as ministry. Nevertheless, in my experience, humans of any or no spirituality need comfort during loss, guidance during life changes, wisdom as they learn, as well as officiants for special occasions like handfastings and marriages. Seekers need leadership which will nurture the best in individuals, raising up new leaders, and where a group coalesces, it needs a compassionate presence willing to serve as a skilled midwife.

If you are a Pagan who wishes to support others in these ways, you will find here a framework for your own work, including stories and examples. If you are an interfaith minister, a chaplain, or a spiritual leader who finds that Pagans are intersecting with your work, you will become acquainted with the culture of this old-but-new spirituality. If you are an educator, you may find *Constellated Ministry* useful in teaching seminarians and students of religious studies.

The very idea of ministry, and terms like ministry, religion, and spirituality, have been hotly contested among Pagans for decades. But ministry is the term of art for what people do when they offer support and leadership to others within a religious framework. No one, to my knowledge, has proffered a better system of language for the work that seems to emerge naturally among groups of the spiritually like-minded. The role of ministry brings to mind the virtually universal tenet of Paganism that all life is connected. Ministry affirms and manifests those connections.

There are no easy answers here; we are attempting to chart a map for a constantly moving starscape. Chapters 1–3 review some history about how we got here, describe spiritual communities and Pagan characteristics, and offer a theory of constellated ministry. Chapter 4 talks to the people who have been ministering to and leading their communities for decades, relating their experiences to our new model. Chapters 5 and 6 contain recommendations, tools and ideas for offering effective Pagan ministry.

Chapter 1

The Changing Landscape of Today's Spiritualities

Declining Group Affiliations

Religious group affiliation has long been the measure by which religious scholars have sought to describe religiosity. Emile Durkheim even went so far as to define religion as the collective sharing of a set of beliefs and practices, ignoring the mystics of every age who have lived within their own idiosyncratic spirituality. Still, religious attendance has been so ubiquitous that it has provided a basis for many studies of its benefits, like lowered mortality, life satisfaction, and a sense of well-being.[6] When Alexis de Tocqueville toured the United States early in the nineteenth century, he famously observed that Americans have tended to belong to organizations which provided structure, belief systems and social ties. People with strong religion-based personal networks are said to be more religiously observant, more sociable, and more likely to have religiously diverse friends than others. Even non-religious group participation has been a constant force. In Europe and

---

6   Conrad Hackett, Joey Marshall, and Anna Schiller, "Religion's Relationship to Happiness, Civic Engagement and Health Around the World," *Pew Research Center*, 2019. https://www.pewforum.org/2019/01/31/religions-relationship-to-happiness-civic-engagement-and-health-around-the-world/.

former European colonies of the last century, the parish most often served as the locus of charitable, war support, educational and other community efforts.

These affiliations have declined, however, over the past fifty years. Individuals now tend to belong to organizations that meet a personal need or interest, rather than joining a common cause for the betterment of the overall community—that is, if they belong to any group at all beyond work and home. Social trust—the belief in the honesty and integrity of other people—has also declined significantly and pervasively in Western societies. Unfortunately, when social ties are loosened, relationships can be weakened by a lack of civility and lack of trust. The introduction noted that individualism carries with it a burden of responsibility to balance self-interest and social commitment. Without the check and balance of group affiliation, individuals must work harder to independently negotiate the terms of a spiritual and ethical life. Group participation (in various types of organizations, including religious groups) is thought to strengthen society, and a lack of group connections appears to weaken community responses to social problems.[7] Some say that religion is both social and organizational, not simply an individual quest, while others—notably in the Pagan world—might insist on the primacy of the individual spiritual journey.

In spite of lessened affiliations, most still claim a religious affiliation or identity of some kind, and many still say they are "looking" for a religion. Even

---

7 Renate Ysseldyk, Kimberly Matheson, and Hymie Anisman, "Religiosity as Identity: Toward an Understanding of Religion From a Social Identity Perspective," *Personality and Social Psychology Review* 14, no. 1 (2010): 60–71.

among those who eschew a religious identity, almost a third say belonging to a community of like-minded people is very important for them. Clearly, a large number of people feel that some sort of religious affiliation is important for them, but just as clearly we can see ambivalence about what that means at a time of steadily shifting population, from a society of belonging, to one of independent pursuits.

Spiritual or Religious?

Some ambivalence around religious identification might be a matter of semiotics, that is, how we create and communicate meaning. The terms "spiritual" and "religious" can have varying meanings for different people. While the majority of Americans identify themselves as both religious and spiritual, Baby Boomers are more likely to say they are spiritual rather than religious. The trend appears to be continuing in subsequent generations.[8] There is some evidence to suggest that the younger you are, the more likely you are to use the word "spiritual" rather than "religious." Answers to the Pagan Engagement survey, as well as other studies, suggest that meanings of the two terms can overlap or even be ambiguous.

When Linda Mercadante interviewed individuals around the United States, she found that the spiritual-but-not-religious, or SBNRs, usually insist that spirituality is personal and religion is institutional, even though that is not a distinction made by researchers.

---

8   Gregory Smith, "America's Changing Religious Landscape," *Pew Research Center's Religion & Public Life Project* (blog), (May 12, 2015), http://www.pewforum.org/2015/05/12/americas-changing-religious-landscape/.

SBNRs tend to be perennialist ("All religions are valid and can be traced to universal truths") and refuse the idea that one religion can have all the answers. Their reasons for leaving formal religions are intensely personal, including theology or matters of personal integrity. They exhibit the very Western tendency towards bricolage of ideas and practices, which is also a Pagan tendency, especially for those who identify as "eclectic." SBNRs emphasize personal experience and personal freedom, seeking acceptance of diversity, non-hierarchical leadership, informality, and theological engagement.[9] This description might be applied to a great majority of contemporary Pagans, with accompanying implications for how Pagans may view religious community similarly to SBNRs or have similar spiritual support needs.

Multiple Religious Identities

Pagans are also found among the growing number of people who identify with more than one religion. Some come to it by birth, say, to an Indian Hindu father and a Sikh mother, or a Catholic mother and a Jewish father. These individuals may grow up attending the services and feast days of both parents' religions. In public, such as grade school, they may avoid identifying with a non-mainstream religion in front of others, or eschew religious identity of any kind, while maintaining a dual devotion at home. Others reject or simply leave behind (e.g., with marriage to a spouse with a new or no faith) the religion of their birth, practice another one for a time, then return to their original religion, bringing

---

9   Linda Mercadante, *Belief without Borders*.

their new practices and beliefs with them. And there are those for whom, as theologian Duane Bidwell says, one religion is not enough. These people, who Bidwell calls "spiritually fluid," have either been raised with or explored several religious identities, ultimately rejecting the restriction of one label. Their exploration may be a life habit, born from curiosity, fed by the enjoyment of learning about others.[10]

Many of these latter wash up on the shores of Paganism, where they find a lack of dogma combined with flexible devotional practices. Although there is a new generation of Pagan-raised young adults emerging, Pagans generally are new to their spirituality. They often blend with Paganism the things that they perceive as the best of the religions and traditions they have tried along the way. Some will have strong emotions attached to the religions they left behind — often negative. But they may also be acculturated to expect the structures of those previous religions, finding themselves confused or even disappointed with the apparent informality or even disorganization they see in Pagan groups or events. Others will be relieved by the lack of expectations of conformity.

The New Shape of Community

Moving another level deeper into the current spiritual landscape, we see significant changes over the past several decades in how people define community, including spiritual or religious community. Redefining

---

10 Duane R. Bidwell, *When One Religion Isn't Enough: Hinjews, Buddhist-Christians, and Other Spiritually Fluid People* (Boston: Beacon Press, 2018).

themselves in relation to ideas of community, individuals have also renegotiated their connections, participation in, and obligations to community and religious groups.

The rise of so-called megachurches in the late twentieth century presented the difficulty of growing close social connections among members who might only see each other at a worship service attended by thousands. The response was to organize as many members and attendees as possible in small groups, sometimes called cell groups, or in later Unitarian Universalist (UU) adaptations, small groups, chalice circles, covenant groups, or wisdom circles. UU congregations have reported dramatic increases in both membership and retention since beginning small group programs.

The small-group movement cannot be understood without some knowledge of the changes in religious life in recent decades. The rise in secularism, individualism, and perception of the central role of spiritual growth provide context for the small-group emphasis on personal responsibility for one's faith. Robert Wuthnow related the egalitarian accessibility of small groups to the American history of disestablishmentarianism (the movement to separate church from state). Small groups have also lessened the authority of clergy and reduced the cost of participation by decreasing the need of physical infrastructure and clergy responsibility. His critique of small groups is that they promote a "me-first" spirituality, with an "anything goes" attitude. He concluded that small groups were not a replacement for other spiritual practices. Despite those misgivings, Wuthnow saw the small groups movement as being so large that it was irrevocably changing American society.[11]

By 2010, Wuthnow was writing about the difficulties of deriving meaning from surveys about religious practice, because as small group practice became a staple for updated congregational ministry it proved more difficult to measure individual religious participation. Most of the small groups in Wuthnow's study were religious, but other researchers found that small group participation did not necessarily lead to a deeper faith, and might even advance the infiltration of secularity into groups. Small groups seem to have been very effective as a strategy for achieving the objectives of religious leaders when they were integrated into wider congregational life. Benefits—such as broader engagement, voluntarism and philanthropy by members—have at times been dramatic, but small groups also can promote an eclectic, individualistic approach to spirituality, with less intense community involvement. Such eclecticism may understandably be seen as weakening the dogma and influence of rigid religious groups.

In contrast to such concerns, Unitarian Universalists (UUs) have found the small group movement to be an antidote to sluggish membership growth and participation. UU congregations organized in small groups have effectively shifted many traditional responsibilities away from the minister, because groups have often filled roles such as pastoral support for their group members. This has helped to alleviate ministerial burnout, but has also forced questions about what a professional minister's work should look like in this

---

[11] Wuthnow, Robert, *I Come Away Stronger: How Small Groups are Shaping American Religion* (Grand Rapids: Eerdmans, 1994), 344–66.

changing environment. Pagan groups have wrestled with aspects of this dilemma for decades as they realized the burdens placed on a volunteer coven priest or priestess. The small group movement closely resembles the traditional small group structure of contemporary Paganism — primarily private meetings in homes, not registered with the state or the tax authority, and with little hierarchy of leadership. Even with the intimacy and flexibility accorded by smaller size, these groups usually lack the cohesion of a paid minister or coordinator, a building to meet in, or an organizational infrastructure to support growth and change.

When people belong to groups with broadly shared values, there is a higher degree of social trust. It's only natural that we would feel more confidence in a person we have gotten to know through our mothers group or while working on a political campaign. But when most of our affiliations are based on having more or less the same opinions, we tend to have less interaction with people different from us — people who might challenge our thinking. Defining themselves oppositionally (e.g., as something other than Christian, or other than their own specific tradition) and being intensely individualistic, Pagans can easily fall into affiliations or group identities that limit the stimulus of diverse interactions. Already existing shared understandings, for example, of nature as divine, the body as sacred, or the legitimacy of a wide spectrum of sexual expression, may be forces for coalescence among some Pagan groups, but the groups may still lack the challenge of varying opinions and interaction by members which is more likely within a place-based group.

A second phenomena in religious life is brought on by email and the internet. It is no longer necessary to physically attend a group gathering in order to participate and benefit from teaching, ritual and friendship with others. Since the mid-1980s religious discussions and practices have emerged online, first through bulletin board discussion lists, and quickly expanding to cyber- and email churches, virtual weddings and other ceremonies, blogging, podcasts and social media platforms and, more recently, mobile applications.

Amidst this proliferation, the struggle to relate online and offline experience can be awkward, with offline often labeled as "real life," as if online experience is somehow false, even though internet users consider both realities part of their whole social life. Even if internet-based ties can be criticized as weak, could it be that weak social ties can lead to stronger ones? In fact, some claim that internet relationships are not at all weaker than offline ones.[12] Certainly, for those with little or no access to a local group, computer and mobile technologies supplement personal social contacts by increasing the ease of meeting and communicating with others. As our aging populations swell, and as new technologies allow those with disabilities to join online communities in new ways, electronic community is bound to grow in importance.

In spite of concerns that the internet might erode or replace social networks, including religious group participation, religious web "surfers" turn out to be the most active offline participants in their faiths. The majority of Americans feel that the internet has a positive impact on religious groups' ability to communicate

---

12 Paul McClure, "Tinkering with Technology and Religion in the Digital Age: The Effects of Internet Use on Religious Belief, Behavior, and Belonging," *Journal for the Scientific Study of Religion* 56, no. 3 (2017): 481–97.

with members, with 79 percent who are active in a religion also being internet users.[13] Gaps in usage between age, educational, racial and regional groups continue to close steadily. Whatever your opinion about their relative merits, the reality of religious life appears to be some synthesis of online and offline experience. It is possible that contemporary society in the developed world, including the Pagan community, is moving closer to viewing online and offline as mutually complementary rather than binary, either-or choices.

Increased Chaplaincies

As former church and synagogue members move into SBNR identities, the field of chaplaincy has grown in size to meet the need for spiritual support in non-religious settings. Today we find chaplains serving not only hospitals, prisons, and hospice facilities, but in legislative bodies, military forces, law enforcement, and in some public schools. There are "corporate chaplains" for large workplaces, chaplains at airports, and even on cruise ships. Disaster response chaplains serve fire and police departments and Red Cross operations. On virtually every college campus in the United States, some kind of chaplaincy program, or a cluster of them, are available to student, faculty and staff. Prisons in the U.S. are required to accommodate the religious needs of inmates, and the armed forces have long been served by soldiers whose duty it was to meet the religious needs of those in the field or on a military base.

---

13   Heidi A. Campbell and Allessandra Vitullo, "Assessing Changes in the Study of Religious Communities in Digital Religion Studies," *Church, Communication and Culture* 1, no. 1 (2016): 73–89.

The wide variety of chaplaincies illustrates a consistent human need for something beyond medical care (including mental health care) when people are in trauma, away from home, or facing unexpected life challenges without the presence of a personal minister or priest. Many of us have experienced the late-night call, or the unexpected ring of the doorbell, by someone who has no religious affiliation but who, when they feel overwhelmed, remembers that we are some kind of spiritual leader whom they trust. At such times, we become a sort of community chaplain, attempting to support someone who may or may not share our spirituality, but for whom we feel compassion. Chapter 3 will say more about chaplaincy as one model for Pagan ministry.

Chapter 2

Who Are Contemporary Pagans?

A Little Background

Without formal structures or membership rolls, it is difficult to quantify the prevalence of Paganism. Wicca, probably the largest Pagan category, is a new religious movement that has grown rapidly in the United Kingdom since the 1950s and in the United States since the 1960s. It quickly spread in the 1950s to the United States, Canada, and continental Europe. Sharp increases in reported numbers of all Pagan religions during the 1980s and 1990s led to contemporary Paganism's recognition as an established movement and an area for academic studies; this growth may have slowed somewhat in the 2010s. In America, it gained considerable traction with the feminist movement, environmentalism, and the growth of interest in New Thought, metaphysical studies, and alternative spiritualities.

There is no uniform definition of what it means to be Pagan, but most forms of contemporary Paganism express a reverence for nature as sacred, with no need to elevate or prioritize an unseen spiritual world or afterlife over earthly existence. Beliefs and practices are characterized by fluidity and flexibility. Many, if not most, contemporary Pagans go beyond nature reverence to animism, acknowledging inherent energy or even sentience in the natural world. Definitions of polytheism vary, but most Pagans would strenuously reject the linear fallacy that monotheism is an evolutionary manifestation of progressive enlightenment. Even tradition names and definitions continue to be contested as the movement struggles to define itself. "Witch" or "Wiccan" has been the most common identification. Other faiths include Druidry, Goddess worship, shaman, Heathenry, Ásatrú, Stregheria, Segnature, or simply Paganism, and many more, as well as various reconstructionist traditions like Hellenic, Kemetic, Afro-Caribbean, and Greco-Roman Paganisms. Close to half of respondents to the Pagan Engagement Survey mentioned witchcraft or Wicca; most respondents mentioned multiple religions and influences.

The term "Pagan" is sometimes contested as being a label applied by scholars, not the name by which individuals choose to identify their religion. It is the generally accepted term in religious studies, so I have chosen to use it throughout this book to refer to members of any of the traditions mentioned above, or to any individual connecting their spirituality to nature or to pre-Abrahamic religions.

Pagan Self-Definition

Being loath to appear conformist, most Pagans eschew labels of any sort. Anyone attempting to discover a neat fit for Pagans in their religious studies is going to be frustrated by the myriad ways in which Pagans either define themselves, or avoid description altogether. A chaplain may find that one person says they are a witch, but that it is not their religion. Another will say her religion is Wicca. Heathens may decline to be called Pagan. Recent years have seen an assertion of difference between Pagans and polytheists (even though many Pagans are polytheist), with an accompanying distinction between hard polytheist and soft polytheist.[14]

More than 1,600 Americans responded to the 2017 Pagan Engagement survey.[15] Collectively, they named more than two hundred traditions or types of Paganism that they practice. When asked to select one category to describe their spirituality (religious, spiritual, humanist, SBNR, none of these) almost two-thirds added an often-lengthy explanation of their beliefs, and more than half wrote in that they identify with their own combination of the choices given, e.g., "I am Humanist and SBNR." Many of the commenters gave a name to their spirituality, such as Gnostic, Hermetic, Theist, Animist, Mystic, Celtic, and Episco-pagan. The apparent reluctance to conform with even the most general of labels given as choices in this survey question suggests a growing fluidity of spiritual identity, parallel to that being observed about religious participation in general, not just Pagan.

Survey comments further sharpened a dichotomy between "religious" and "spiritual," voicing a perception that the word "religion" signals control, manipulation, dogma, insincerity, and even abuse. The implication was that "spiritual" somehow avoids these traps, as if they are unique to established or institutionalized religions.

---

14   Polytheism is the belief in multiple deities. "Hard" polytheism is the idea that each of the deities is a distinct individual. "Soft" polytheism is the idea that the gods are various manifestations of the same deity, or archetypes of a monistic source.
15   Emore, "Group or Solitary."

Whatever they may call themselves, contemporary Pagans have demonstrated a remarkable pioneering spirit with their constant search for meaning, research of ancient and indigenous ways, and willingness to experiment until they determine a workable theology and practice. Pagan spiritual pioneers may even represent the leading edge of cultural change as they reject stale institutions and embrace fresh approaches to human spiritual experience.

Common Characteristics

Contemporary Pagans are most typically non-hierarchical. Many religions feature a hierarchy of leadership which urges conformity to norms such as membership and group participation. These authorities ostensibly derive their authority from a divine source or a divinely transmitted text, or at least from a succession of authority (e.g., a bishop). Pluralism, the belief that diverse ideas can coexist peacefully, has forced many religious groups to reinterpret religious authority, in some cases favoring individual freedom of choice over obedience to an institution. Even given this evolution towards a blend of institutional authority and individual autonomy, most religious individuals can point to a source of their beliefs or practices. But Pagans do not view sacred texts as authoritative; Pagan priests have no inherent authority over group members, being primarily trained to lead ceremonies. With no requirement to obey an outside authority, Pagans are free to adopt a solitary practice, determine their own code of ethical behavior, and develop personalized devotional practices.

Pagans tend to be intensely individualistic, frequently holding countercultural attitudes,[16] and being mistrustful of authority and structures, particularly religious. These are values which lend strength to a growing movement, but when out of balance they can also erode group stability. For decades, studies have found that Pagan groups are usually small and unstable. Reasons for group failure are many, but with fluid work and living situations, there is increasing instability because of members who move away, have child-related needs, or simply move on in their spiritual search, either to a different religion or to become one of the nones.

Aside from a personal preference for being solitary, the most significant Pagan group impediments are internal conflicts and leadership weaknesses. Conflict has been a consistent undercurrent in Pagan communities since their beginnings, some even earning the widely used term "witch wars." Uneasy sectarian discord between traditionalist and eclectic Pagans has occurred around issues of legitimacy and authority. Traditionalist witches, for example, establish membership and leadership through the succession of a lineage. Formerly secret practices became public when Gardnerian witch Raymond Buckland began publishing around 1970, closely followed in 1971 by Lady Sheba (née Jessie Wicker Bell). Then the influence of Pagan eclecticism following Scott Cunningham's publication of books for solitary practitioners in the 1980s legitimized self-study and self-initiation for many.

---

16 Chas S. Clifton, *Her Hidden Children: The Rise of Wicca and Paganism in America* (Lanham, Md.: AltaMira Press 2006).

Tension between individualism and embrace of spiritual community can precipitate sharp disagreements, with members leaving a group. Additionally, there are unconfirmed but widespread reports of disaffection by some Pagans who avoid groups after experiencing sexual harassment. Conflict between and among groups erodes valuable community ties, creating polarization, until community members withdraw from any participation. It's also a significant factor for many Pagans' choice to be solitary, signaling the importance of developing strategies for better communications and enhanced civility in Pagan groups.

Pagans have historically felt the need for secrecy, still troubled by ghosts of the past, from the Inquisition, to the Grimm Brothers' tales, to the more recent Satanic panic.[17] Fear of exposure compels many to choose solitary practice, to prevent harassment of their children at school, or bias against them at work. Some Pagan religious groups, such as witchcraft and Wicca, have used initiations and oaths to guard what they consider arcane or hidden knowledge. Others insist on secrecy as simply a matter of privacy. Unfortunately, when Pagans adopt a concealment strategy to protect themselves from prejudice, this can lead to stress, but exposure can have more serious consequences, like hindered career achievement or loss of child custody.

Most respondents to the 1999 Pagan Census[18] said that they wanted to see Paganism become more

---

17 'Satanic panic' is the term used for a conspiracy theory which gained traction in the 1980s and 1990s alleging the ritual abuse and murder of thousands by occult practitioners.
18 Helen A. Berger, Evan A. Leach, and Leigh S. Shaffer, *Voices from the Pagan Census: A National Survey of Witches and Neo-Pagans in the United States* (Columbia, S.C.: University of South Carolina Press, 2003).

mainstream, perhaps hoping for acceptance and safety within mainstream culture. Others were willing to remain marginal, seeing churches and the development of hierarchy as a threat to the radical nature of their religion. These seemingly opposite points of view lead to a divide between Pagans who lean towards group institutionalization and those who fear the loss of spiritual autonomy and an egalitarian group structure and practice. Some, such as Wiccans, continue to value group participation in a coven, rather than as a solitary. But access to such a group may not exist, particularly for those in rural areas or small towns. Concerns about privacy or even safety may also inhibit outreach in the search for Pagan spiritual support or community.

The Pagan tendency to distrust authority might contribute to the prominent role of occult stores as centers of Pagan community and sources of learning, places where there is no formal spiritual authority. One need not belong to a group or attend a congregation in order to learn about spirituality and feel spiritual. This is very different from the early Wiccan model of a coven leader who trains and initiates group members. Commodification can easily come to replace personal growth, impersonal consumer exchanges substituting for authentic spiritual practice. Solitary practice informed primarily by commodified spirituality could lead someone to overlook the benefit of group affiliation. The commercialization of religion and spirituality manifests not just in Pagan/occult stores, but also in Christian, New Age, and ethnically based stores, paid workshops and products related to spirituality.

The past three decades have seen a dramatic rise in commodified Pagan material culture as evidenced in Pagan book and media publishing, sales of Pagan-themed jewelry, clothing and ritual items, fees for workshops and events, and online Pagan-themed stores. Consumerism reduces authoritarian influence and changes the nature of social bonds since its ultimate intended outcome is profit, spiritual purpose being a side benefit. Thus, an individual may purchase a pentacle necklace and a how-to book of spells and then identify as Pagan, with no further training and no nurturing by knowledgeable community groups. A Pagan store may function as a social hub and source of training, but has an inherent, if mild, conflict of interest when it comes to being a sole source of spiritual community.

Anthropologist Sabina Magliocco has noted important parallels between Paganism and American democracy, saying, "The tension between the desire for community and the desire for individualism is a central leitmotif in American Pagan culture, reflecting the presence of these twin conflicting desires in the surrounding dominant culture of the United States."[19] This is a puzzling tension, juxtaposed as it is with the recent predominance of Pagan solitary practice, prompting a return to the questions about why Pagans are affiliated or unaffiliated. The persistence of Pagan individualism poses an additional question as to whether it may reflect the same tendency in those who identify themselves as "spiritual but not religious" or SBNR, since Pagan solitaries have increased during the same years that mainstream religious congregations have experienced a marked decline in membership and participation.

---

19 Sabina Magliocco, *Witching Culture: Folklore and Neo-Paganism in America* (Philadelphia: University of Pennsylvania Press, 2010), 60.

The reasons for and prevalence of group affiliation and solitary practice are important to understand when we attempt to define best practices for ministry. Helen Berger once discussed the growth of solitary Pagan practice in an online article reviewing early findings of her Pagan Census Revisited compared to the original Pagan Census.[20] While her data showed that Pagans who claim to be solitary had risen to 79 percent, up from 51 percent in the earlier study, she did not find this to be an indicator of social isolation, but rather of the wide availability of how-to books and the internet. She reported that most of these practitioners meet with other Pagans at least annually, or as often as monthly, for spiritual activities and as often as weekly or daily for social reasons. In her latest publication Berger notes that solitaries are rarely isolated, but most now participate in new ways of social integration, including the internet. These social ties, however fine the threads, are important to the concept of ministry proposed by this book.

Festival participation shows the ongoing desire for meaningful community and a sense of belonging which can only take place when large groups of people with shared values come together. Thousands of Pagans attend the frequent large festivals and conferences with great enthusiasm. Of those who regularly attend these annual gatherings, some report their participation as a group affiliation, although their personal practice is solitary or sporadic the rest of the year. Community then becomes an occasionally linked group of individuals, connected by shared values or beliefs, but without

---

[20] This revised census formed the basis of Berger's book *Solitary Pagans: Contemporary Witches, Wiccans, and Others Who Practice Alone* (Columbia, S.C.: University of South Carolina Press, 2019).

physical access to each other through a common neighborhood or region.

The general shift away from place-based community in America and beyond to some extent reflects widespread disquiet and ambivalence regarding the authenticity of new blended spiritualities. Paganism falls squarely within the concept of blended spirituality, although Pagans nevertheless often obsess over lineage of tradition, and authenticity as validated by pre-Abrahamic historical paganisms. Modernization and globalization are forces that uproot traditions; those very forces generate strong Pagan longings for wisdom with a pedigree, for example, because of its antiquity. Pagans have long-embraced what they (usually idealistically) imagine to have been pre-Christian cultures, such as Celtic, Hellenic, Germanic, Norse, Mesopotamian and Indus Valley.

In short, any approach to Pagan ministry must take into account the following factors characteristic of many Pagans:

- Tension between desires for individualism and community
- Mistrust of authority and hierarchy
- Still-nascent and evolving definitions of Pagan religions and spiritualities
- Wide misunderstanding of Pagans by society
- Desire for at least periodic gatherings in tandem with preference for being solitary
- Need for validation of religious authenticity
- Secrecy about being Pagan
- Lack of broadly accepted standards and training for Pagan leaders

Against these vulnerabilities stands an enviable phalanx of strengths:

- Open to new ideas, eager to learn
- Highly creative
- Adaptable to change
- Tolerant of other religions
- Uninterested in converting others to Paganism
- Link self-empowerment to service to others[21]

Unique Culture and Spiritual Needs

Life passages such as marriage, birth, death, coming of age, and divorce, bring most of us to look around for a helping hand, whatever our religion. Celebration of joys, companionship in grief, and comfort during trouble are universal; few of us navigate these times alone. Pagans often face additional challenges unique to their culture. In many places, one's religion still conveys social acceptance, even the cachet of membership in a privileged group. The possibility of workplace discrimination or harassment invokes fear for most Pagans, who are still thought of as godless or evil by too many of their coworkers. Despite the protection of non-discrimination policies and federal law, revealing one's Paganism, even inadvertently, can bring serious consequences such as attempts by others to convert, being overlooked for promotion, or downright harassment.

When it comes to anything involving children and family, Pagans have typically been at a strong disadvantage. Only a few years ago I was brought in as a sort of expert to advise and mediate in a custody case. During

---

21 Ibid., 95.

my meeting with the child's mother, a social worker, and a law enforcement officer, I answered many questions about witchcraft. After nearly an hour, it became clear that although the professionals in the room held no bias against Paganism, the mother was determined to use her husband's Pagan religion against him in her divorce in order to deny him access to their child.

In another case shared with me, a husband and wife couple, both in law enforcement, were longtime Wiccans. During their divorce, the husband claimed his wife was unfit as a mother because she was a witch. The court awarded him sole custody of their children, all of this while the wife continued to work as a sworn officer of the law. It took nearly ten years for her to regain some kind of custodial rights to her own children.

While mainstream Christian denominations have regularly foundered in the shoals of whether to support same-sex marriages, such relationships have been present among American Pagans from the beginning. (Notable exceptions might be the early years of British Traditional Witchcraft and some more conservative Heathen groups.) Pagan ministers have often been sought out for gay or lesbian handfastings since they are accepting of such relationships. Pagans are also, for the most part, supportive of polyamorous relationships, committed triads (or more) of individuals. Polyamory is a common enough practice among some Pagans, but they must again be cautious because of the perception that they are only indulging in promiscuous behavior. If one member of the group is a parent, this is particularly problematic. The need to protect their same-sex or polyamorous family reinforces the culture of secrecy already so prevalent among Pagans.

Because of these vulnerabilities, a minister supporting Pagans will find it essential to establish trust, demonstrate respect for varying or even mutable beliefs, and be willing to serve as a reliable spiritual companion during sensitive times.

Most of those who responded to the Pagan Engagement Survey expressed a desire for support from a trained leader in exploring and going deeper with their spirituality. Nearly half indicated a desire for support during life passages such as weddings and funerals, and life stresses such as employment, family or health issues. More than a third desired support in learning about their own tradition. Only 6.4 percent said they had no spiritual needs at all.[22]

These four categories encompass a variety of services for which a Pagan might look to a minister. These include teaching, mentoring, officiating special ceremonies, and pastoral counseling, in addition to the more commonly assumed role of leading ritual. Many individuals derive comfort from receiving these supports from someone they feel is rooted in the same or a similar spiritual path, and who has the training to provide higher quality, ethical and competent ministry.

---

22 Holli Emore, *Group or Solitary: Choice and Spiritual Care Needs in Contemporary Paganism* (Columbia, S.C.: Cherry Hill Seminary, 2018), 54.

Chapter 3

A New Ministry Model

Moving Past Assumptions

What might the Pagan ministry of the future look like? For that matter, there is *ministry*, and there is the person who performs that work, the *minister*. Pagans have debated for years what they want and need of their spiritual leaders. Should they be called by names which have been used by the Christian mainstream culture for centuries? What is the relevance of initiation to priesthood? What about the "priesthood of all"? Who gets to say how a Pagan group functions? To what extent should Pagans conform to public expectations about clergy in order to legally perform marriages or visit prisons? What determines the borders of someone's ministry? Would a minister serve a particular place-based group? A locale or region? A niche of social media followers or a virtual-only group? Or would a minister be attached to a group at all? To whom should a Pagan minister make herself available?

Some Pagans further maintain a demarcation between the role of a priest—one initiated into a tradition and leading rituals, and a minister—one who serves the broader spiritual needs of people. Training for leadership in many Pagan traditions has until recently primarily stressed ritual skills and willingness or ability to train others in the tradition. Others give prominence to scholarship and religious history studies—Druid groups, for example. A practice of purely personal devotion to deity or deities is common for many Pagans, but particularly for those who consider themselves solitary. Then there are those suspicious of routinization or standardization of Pagan practices, who look askance at anything that reminds them of the religions they rejected.

To those worried about the so-called Protestantization of Paganism, I would point out that spiritual care support in the form of professional chaplains now comes from Buddhists, Muslims, Sikhs, Hindus, and atheists. Ministry need not be defined by the religious affiliation of the minister or support person, nor serve as a function of only a specific religion. Rather, I suggest that when Pagans step into ministerial work, they bring a unique worldview to the care they provide. Furthermore, the spiritual needs of the Pagan community will be best understood and therefore best served by its own practitioners.

I do not expect Pagans to begin financially supporting trained ministers in my lifetime. Most people currently doing the work of supporting Pagan spirituality are at the grassroots level, holding down a job or career to support themselves. The Christian world, also struggling to adapt to changing times (including falling numbers), calls this "tentmaking," a reference to the apostle Paul's working trade. I have a colleague who refers to himself as an "at-large" rabbi, not attached to a congregation, but quite busy. At the same time, many mainstream religion seminary students in the United States are graduating into a society unlikely to ever employ them in a manner that will pay off their student debt.

A New Ministry Model

Nearly every Pagan group leader or priest seems to have a "day job" to pay the bills. Many of these have expressed to me the fatigue of filling dual roles, with only one role generating an income. Add to this Pagans' generally dubious outlook about material support for spiritual services, and the future does not look good for any kind of recognizable, sustainable ministry. Old ideas about ministry may keep some Pagans stuck between a perceived past and a desired future, creating barriers to growth. Progress will require some soul-searching and creative re-visioning in the Pagan community.

Two assumptions from the past strike me as particularly relevant. First, Pagans can be fiercely independent while simultaneously expecting at least occasional benefits from a supportive community. The kind of uncooperative individualism to which many Pagans cling prevents cultivation of healthy affiliations, and even undermines well-intentioned efforts with dissension, burnout or just plain apathy. Anyone with a talent for ministry might be daunted by such ambivalence towards the gifts they offer.

The second assumption derives from our society, including most Pagans, having long been imprinted with the last century's definition of clergy. We still confuse the vocation with the career. As desirable as it might be to have professionally trained clergy who are adequately compensated for organizing, maintaining, inspiring and teaching a congregation, Pagans either don't have the numbers or the will to support such positions. Lack of financial support for a minister, however, does not eliminate the need for spiritual support, nor does it invalidate the person with a desire to pursue ministry as a vocation. We also tend to think of a minister as one individual following a linear career trajectory, even while we acknowledge that the job is too big for any person alone.

Each of these assumptions can be crippling, but I believe there is a way out of the woods, by re-envisioning the concept of ministry, adjusting the telescope, if you will, to bring into focus a starscape we've been unable to see in the past.

Interconnection — Interdependence

The forces of globalization are constantly examined by economic experts and sociologists. Most of us follow the logic of arguments for and against moving corporate operations overseas, or the risks of trade tariffs, for example. But globalization steadily and increasingly transforms our local communities, too, propelled by immigration, rapid worldwide communication, and the mobility afforded by non-farming. The truth is, we are already immersed in a global society, it's just that we are now more aware of it than ever before in human history.

An important part of globalization is exposure to other religions. Religion — not just our own — powerfully shapes us. Our children learn in school that their new friend doesn't believe in Jesus. The couple down the street invite us to a quinceañera Mass and party for their daughter. At Chanukah, we hear of how Jewish families teach their offspring to be intentionally charitable. In my own small suburban neighborhood, a former Assembly of God church has been bought by a Hindu group; now we enjoy the delight of nearby fireworks at Divali and Holi.

Religion professor Kevin Minister writes that one of the ways we experience global realities locally is through a dense web in which religions are "networked, interrelated phenomena embedded in local communities and cultures."[23] The general public often sees itself as inhabiting a dominant mainstream religious culture, especially if they are part of that mainstream faith. In reality, spirituality is far from uniform, and our communities more nearly resemble a tapestry of multicolored interwoven threads.

If Pagans understand anything, it is the complexity of interconnected reality. As a so-called "earth religion," Paganism was an early adopter of the Gaia environmental principle. Pagans celebrate physical embodiment as part of the ecosystem; they do not aspire to a superior afterlife or nonphysical reality. They similarly embrace diversity as a natural manifestation of our social ecosystem, most of them celebrating the cultural and religious globalism of the current century.

For centuries, religious congregations have built site-specific ministries: sanctuaries, chapels, shrines, monasteries, synagogues, and grottos. Meanwhile, most traditions of American contemporary Pagans have demonstrated intentional portability, holding circles in backyards, woods and fields, parks, or living rooms. Neither way is wrong, but we can see that church buildings everywhere are being sold to theaters, restaurants and condo developers because their dwindling memberships could no longer support the upkeep. At the same time, Pagans of late are less willing to put up with

---

23 Kevin Minister, "Transforming Introductory Courses in Religion: From World Religions to Interreligious Studies," in *Interreligious/Interfaith Studies: Defining a New Field*, eds. Eboo Patel, Jennifer Howe Peace, and Noah J. Silverman (Boston: Beacon Press, 2018), 62.

the inconveniences of meeting in the wild, or advertising personal addresses and opening their homes to strangers, but have little to no existing spaces to serve as suitable public alternatives.

In a systems approach, at least two groups have noted the lessening relevance of traditional places of ministry, and the rise of unaffiliated individuals who prefer to access spiritual support on their own terms. The Chaplaincy Innovation Lab and Fetzer Institute recently released a report[24] which discusses the need for "demand-centered" chaplaincy, one contributor saying....

> As major studies on the current religious landscape have outlined, more and more Americans are stepping away from traditional understandings of religion and are increasingly absent from the traditional spaces in which religion has been practiced. Despite this, the need for making meaning out of an increasingly chaotic world and one's place in it is a need that will not go away.
>
> Chaplains must look to humankind's expressed needs and be nimble in our abilities to meet those needs in innovative ways and in nontraditional spaces. This question of how the work of chaplaincy must change with the changing demographic landscape of the United States is a crucial one. To be rigid in this regard will lead to the field's obsolescence.[25]

Although the report speaks of chaplains, the function and concerns of a chaplain are entirely apropos to the considerations of ministry to Pagans.

---

24 Wendy Cadge and Michelle A. Scheidt, "Meditations on Chaplaincy and Spiritual Care: A Conversation with Chaplains Across Settings." Chaplaincy Innovation Lab and Fetzer Institute (2020), http://chaplaincyinnovation.org/resources/meditations.

25 Ibid., 11.

Gravitational Theory

There has been less discussion among Pagans about the interrelation of which Kevin Minister writes. If they are widely dispersed, or assembling only on special occasions like festivals or a particular holy day, Pagans are nonetheless firmly embedded in their communities, workplaces, and schools. Religiously distinct, their lives are very much part of Minister's complexity. Awareness of embeddedness in overlapping segments of society is intrinsic to the new theory of ministry described in this book. As many as 80 percent of Pagans say they are solitary, but virtually all of those are still stakeholders and participants in any number of groups, both real-world and virtual. The boundaries, meanings and memberships of such groups fluctuate continually. At no time, however, do we live in a void. The rub comes with trying to find each other.

A gravitational theory of philosophy suggests that like-minded people are somehow drawn to each other in affinity groups, be they friendships, clubs, or political parties.[26] Gravitational theory sounds metaphysical, but appears to manifest so regularly that it has attracted wide application in economics, political science, and other fields. It is important to us because we are interested in the people who feel a spiritual gravitational pull. Pagan ministers might use the concept to better understand how to be accessible to what are often transitory or even fleeting populations.

Marketers draw on gravitational theory when they look at the relative benefits of push or pull marketing.

---

26 George Berkeley, "Moral Attraction," in Alexander Campbell Fraster, *The Works of George Berkeley Volume 3* (London: Macmillan, 1861), 189.

"Push" marketing mainly looks at products (and how to push them to the buyer), whereas "pull" marketing attempts to draw customers based on a shared purpose or desire. Attempting to push a service, a Pagan teaching group, for example, where there is simply no interest or need, just won't work. When we pay attention to the subjects being mentioned by those in our community and identify interest in a discussion group or special program, that's using pull marketing. Marketers then get to work pulling potential users together using what the industry calls *engagement platforms*. Unique combinations of strategies, from social media, to coupons, media interviews, and corporate charity, comprise engagement platforms. (Chapter 5 will discuss how combined strategies become a ministry tool, or a ministry constellation.)

We see social gravitation at work when people are drawn to a faith congregation. Gathering from randomly scattered locations, people in a congregation nevertheless relate to each other based on their religion. Participation in the religion grows resulting bonds of social gravity. But each of these individuals is part of countless other networks, the points of interaction ranging as widely as do individual members' interests.

Another way of thinking about how we find each other is *communities of practice,* a concept developed in the 1990s about the ways that people learn outside of a formal educational environment.[27] Communities of practice tend to be informal, task- or interest-oriented and temporary, only lasting until the original purpose is fulfilled. Many Pagan groups could be thought of as a community of practice, particularly those which

27 Jean Lave and Etienne Wenger, *Situated Learning: Legitimate Peripheral Participation* (Cambridge: Cambridge University Press, 1991).

emphasize teaching. In this light, a Pagan group that winds down after a few years resembles a community of practice that has completed its objectives. The group is not a failed attempt because perpetuity was not the goal. It may even decide to shift its focus to a new purpose that is shared by those already in the group.

Shifting From Place To Function

The neighborhood synagogue or church has long been an icon for religious life, implying that the building is the locus of faith, and burdening rabbis, ministers, and lay leaders with a responsibility for maintaining a decreasingly used physical plant. Researchers of religious trends have shown clearly that religious participation has both decreased and dramatically changed from congregational membership to practice of individual personal spirituality. As society has changed from localized affiliations to highly fluid affinity-based associations, many of them distant or virtual (online), most religious groups and services have done little to adjust, including Pagan groups and leaders.

Until the last century or so, the period when many of our current expectations about religious affiliation and ministry congealed, most people were still close to, or only steps removed from, rural agricultural and small-town life. They expected to remain in one job and one marriage for a lifetime, and join, volunteer for, and make charitable gifts to local organizations, including religious congregations. Ministry methods have, therefore, been developed around the existence of local affiliations and relationship ties. Even witchcraft covens of the last century relied on geographic proximity, group meetings, and individual interactions among members.

Only the widespread availability of online access since the 1990s has altered this pattern.

Pagans often express a desire to be part of a Pagan group, but probably vary in their perceptions and definitions of what is meant by group participation and affiliation. Those who answered the Pagan Engagement survey were asked about their local site-based memberships. Mixed in with clearly defined kindred, coven, and goddess circle memberships were more than a few people who cited a yearly festival, quarterly public ritual, or connection to a Facebook page as their group. Factors like frequency of attendance, used by researchers to measure religiosity, would hardly be relevant with these Pagans.

Covens and groves emerge year after year, then quickly disappear. Sadly, the biggest factors in attrition are internal conflict and poor leadership. Some of these problems can be addressed with for example, leadership and communications training to improve group dynamics. Other barriers to participation are practical, e.g., transportation needs, or disability, and some members may require special support to accommodate a mental health condition, or other special need. Pagans also lament their apparent inability to create their own physical infrastructures. There are notable exceptions: Earthspirit, Circle Sanctuary, Ardantane, New Alexandrian Library, the (Sekhmet) Temple of Goddess Spirituality, or the Goddess Temple of Orange County. But for the most part, attempts to organize shared community centers founder quickly, perhaps illustrating the strength of Pagan cultural individualism and avoidance of hierarchy more than a lack of funds.

Then there are the ubiquitous and longstanding solitaries, the upwards of 80 percent of Pagans who have no group affiliation. Sixty-eight percent of solitaries responding to the Pagan Engagement Survey said they would like to be part of a group, if it were possible and a good fit. Still, many have no choice in the matter, being homebound, or limited by health concerns, or having no access to a close-by group. Others choose solitary practice, finding emotional safety and individual freedom in their spiritual privacy. For solitaries, a place-centric model of ministry is largely irrelevant. To receive outside support, they need the ability to readily access reliable resources.

Similarly, in the 2000s Pagan spirituality in Australia appeared to shift from local-based groups to a combination of Internet communications, occasional group meetings, and less frequent but larger events like festivals. Australian researcher Angela Coco described this as Pagan "networked individualism," an overall reconfiguration of social relationships through internet communications. Pagan communities of practice generated by online connections, she noted, can bring about a sense of belonging not afforded by offline connections. Coco articulated a compelling vision of the Pagan community as "a web of interactive nodes in online and offline places."[28] A vision of networked individualism neither disparages the loss of former group affiliation patterns, nor promotes new ones, but provides for at least this one religion a valuable new map of the religious terrain.

---

28 Angela Coco, "Pagan Religiousness as 'Networked Individualism,'" in *Spirituality: Theory, Praxis and Pedagogy*, eds. Robert Fisher and Daniel Riha (Leiden: Brill, 2012), 125–36.

Constellated Ministry

Using Coco's ideas as a springboard, I propose a new theory of "constellated ministry," which acknowledges the dramatic changes in Pagan affiliations. Affiliations of the past have often been driven by a visionary individual leader, rather than by the social gravitational pull of an idea embodied in a ministry. The leader in this new paradigm would be able to discern the patterns of Pagan network nodes as one would make out the constellation of Orion in the sky.

As an example, a picture of one Pagan's network might include this hypothetical constellation of affinities: training and initiations in two different traditions; a desire to engage in both corporate and solitary religious practices; health needs which discourage or prohibit long walks to an isolated ritual location; a love of group singing; enjoyment and habit of lifelong learning; interest in ancient history; amateur birdwatching and naturalist activities; passion for LGBTQ rights; concern for urban revitalization; and interest in local voluntarism. These interests and needs represent points of entry, or interactive nodes, for a Pagan minister's potential engagement with this sample individual.

Some nodes may overlap: perhaps, walking and group singing with a local senior center by an ad hoc group of local Pagans from various traditions. That same group may join with other Pagan groups for occasional joint rituals and workshops, or offer themselves as choral backup for a special community ritual. The individual may pursue learning about Minoan culture through an online course where she meets people from various states, plus Canada, Belgium, Lebanon, and Italy, in the process discovering a Lebanese person

A New Ministry Model

interested in Canaanite religions who wishes to stay in touch and share ritual ideas. As someone interested in bettering her society, this person has many online connections to social justice advocates in her community. When there is an important rally, calls to be made to elected officials, or a need for workers at an emergency shelter, she turns to her online Pagan network with a call for action, or simply to share information. She may hold a Pagan learning group in her home for a year, to explore leadership issues with local Pagan leaders. She is subscribed to the blog and email list of a Pagan leader she respects, and knows from past experience that she can reach out to this person with questions. Note that each of these nodes is a point of bidirectional interaction, that is, some interaction is initiated by the individual, and other interactions originate externally.

Where in this map does ministry occur? If most Pagans are solitary, and if most have personal needs with which they may desire spiritual support, the network nodes must serve as new entry points for giving and receiving that support. Ministry must consist of a constellation of nodes by which trained leadership and those who desire support may access each other, both actively and passively. Effective ministry and spiritual support of Pagans will involve a combination of online contact, local activities, and occasional special events like public rituals, conferences, and social events, in other words, engagement platforms.

Constellated ministry is a response to the crumbling of old icons such as a charismatic leader who must be visited in a particular place. Pagans who wish to serve as ministers will need to apply their insights about interconnection to find new ways to sustain viable spiritual communities, with or without buildings or paid positions. One conceptual shift is to veer away from the lone-minister profile towards a more collaborative team approach to ministry, or a *leadership constellation*. This is not simply allocating grove tasks to different individuals. It's more about a small group of capable leaders pooling their ministry assets in order to serve their various ministries more effectively while engaging in mutual support. We will come back to leadership constellations in Chapter 5.

Those who wish to offer spiritual support or ministry to Pagans will develop communication channels by which they may be easily accessed. Such channels must respect the autonomy and privacy of Pagans or others who choose to contact a Pagan minister or leader for assistance. With less than half a percent of Pagans in industrialized countries lacking internet access, online and phone communications will be an important component of communication channels. Websites, social media pages, and online listings, will facilitate passive ministry, allowing leaders to respond to those who request support. Web content pushed by feeds, podcasts, YouTube channels, online courses, and webinar presentations and meetings can facilitate active ministry initiated by a Pagan leader.

Online connection became even more important in 2020 when the novel coronavirus forced most of us to restrict our activities. Many people offering mental health services, spiritual direction-mentoring, or spiritual support were already providing these services online. They have weathered stay-at-home orders because access to them was not limited to an office setting.

An additional way to actively provide support to the Pagan community is to develop widely available curricula for study that clarify traditions, teach the skills noted in education and training recommendations below, and provide extended education about related topics, e.g., history of a region and culture which inspired a tradition, or reading and discussion of world sacred texts. Such curricula could provide guidance and structure for CUUPS[29] groups, ADF groves and proto-groves, independent circles and covens, prison Pagan groups, and more. These activities, like spiritual support, can be provided through distance learning, employing online technology

A Pagan cultural move away from secrecy will be important for leaders and groups. Leaders should respect the privacy or confidentiality of individuals, but lurking out of sight has damaged Pagan credibility, depriving Pagans of the benefits of their own local communities. To be effective, I cannot overemphasize the need for deliberate cultivation of community ties, both intrafaith (within Pagan communities) and interfaith (relationships with leaders and members of other religions), as well as various local and regional organizations which may be good allies or project partners (e.g., a food bank or the riverkeeper). Local community ties can prove to be valuable resources during a crisis, or when local Pagan individuals and groups do not have sufficient critical mass to be effective in a cause. Partnerships with non-Pagans can go a long way towards alleviating fears that still prevent many Pagans from participating in open events or keep them from revealing their religion to a hospital chaplain, police officer or victim advocate. Partnerships with both Pagan and non-Pagan community groups can

---

29 Covenant of Unitarian Universalist Pagans.

improve and enrich mutual understanding between groups which previously misunderstood each other.

In summary, constellated ministry replaces the old notions of spiritual support concentrated on one leader or location. It develops the skill of recognizing patterns of affinity and affiliation, builds spiritual engagement platforms, cultivates horizontal leadership across network nodes, and provides accessibility to spiritual support through multiple nodes and leadership collaboration. In the next section, we will learn from some longtime Pagan leaders' experiences.

Chapter 4

Stories From Pagan Leaders

The good news is that many Pagan leaders are already doing work which might easily be called constellated ministry. In most places, the constellations have grown organically, and though some may have lacked a plan for growth or continuity, they have been demonstrably successful. Interviews with individuals around the country about their own experiences helped to illustrate commonalities, concerns, and leadership methods across varied Pagan traditions. About twenty-five individuals from around the country participated in individual interviews with me over a two-year period. Our conversations explored leaders' motivations for ministry, the ways they have made themselves available, what support is sought from them, and how they have dealt with organizational issues, burnout, and the conflicting demands of ministry, family and work.

Leadership Evolution

With little exception, the people I interviewed did not start out seeking a leadership role. The responsibility was an evolutionary process emanating from a desire to help others with similar spiritual interests. In this respect, Pagan leaders are distinctly different from a traditional Christian pastor or priest who attends college, then seminary, then is placed in a congregation by a religious authority. Nor are they expected to undergo intensive theological and textual study such as that found in a yeshiva or madrassa. No one that I met with indicated that they had planned to be head of a group. More often, they expressed reluctance to single themselves out as exceptional; rather, they asserted that they grew into their role out of necessity. I might suggest that they possessed inherent leadership abilities to begin with, but this did not feature in self-characterization of their work.

Typical was this reply to the question, "Do you consider yourself a leader, or do others?" Volunteer hospital chaplain and Wiccan Maggie Beaumont of New Jersey hesitated before answering, "Other people consider me a leader; once in a while I do." Dana Doerksen of Greensong CUUPS in Seattle, Washington, where she also serves on the Board of Trustees, said, "Probably yeah, I guess so." Doerksen says she asked a friend on one occasion, why did you come to me? She wondered if people assumed that because she was a leader of her group, it was her job to be available for counseling and support, "like Christian ministers," even though the leaders were unpaid and did not always have adequate time to respond. Doerksen has been frequently contacted for support by local Pagans. Even so, like Beaumont, her initial response was, "[W]hat people ask me, I do," meaning her own ministry style is one of action, not based on a public understanding of her position, perceived or otherwise.

Archdruid Jean Pagano of Ár nDraíocht Féin (Irish for "Our own Druidry") takes seriously the importance of bringing along new leadership, pointing out that someone is not a leader if no one knows you. He watches the many ADF communities worldwide to identify people who may have leadership potential. Pagano encourages them initially to pursue education and training. He then introduces them to as many others as he is able, believing that by building connections, their leadership potential will grow and express itself in ways that strengthen the community. Pagano says that in ADF it is said that the initiate is the path of one, and clergy is the path of many, making a distinction between the role of ritual leader or psychopomp, and the pastoral role of supporting groups and individuals in their daily lives.

Addressing the topic of leadership, Rev. Karen Andersen of First Unitarian Church in New Bedford (Massachusetts), also a witch, similarly looks for ways to support new leaders. She says, "I have leadership skills; others certainly look to me as a leader. I really like to be the kind of leader that helps other people to lead. I'm enough of a leader to let other people lead." She feels that being the oldest of five children growing up has meant leading from a young age. She echoes Pagano's emphasis on community connections, saying, "I make myself very accessible. Anyone in my coven or congregation know they can drop by my house, call me any time ... I try to be kind and understanding and patient and listen."

Rob Schreiwer, Steersman of The Troth, and founder of Urglaawe tradition, a denomination of Heathenry that is inspired by the Pennsylvania Dutch culture, speaks of his own habit of empowering others. "I like to let people develop what they want, then I give input if I'm needed." Vicki Riffe, a witch in southern Maryland, is part of an eclectic Wiccan group, Nomadic Chantry Tradition, and has a similar philosophy about leadership. "I encourage them [those who attend her classes or who join her coven] to go out and explore." Riffe also emphasizes the need for leaders to cultivate independent thinking and even autonomy in her students. "I don't need a bunch of mini-me's. I don't need a bunch of followers. I'm doing my job and I'm happiest when they have found their spirituality, whatever that is, then I'm at peace, then I'm happy."

Cherry Hill Seminary student Cynthia Cebuhar of Phoenix, Arizona, identifies as Wiccan and Druid, and echoes the others' leadership style of empowering others. She is enthusiastic about her work in her community, and describes her gradual involvement with Phoenix Pagan Pride (PPD) as intentional and strategic. Because of her passion for learning, Cebuhar wanted to support her PPD's workshops. She relates, "Last year I kind of struggled with getting people ... I had a lot of ideas, but people didn't know me. But this year people were knocking on my door trying to get my attention." She continues, "You have to show up, you have to do the work, you have to be welcoming. People will say to me, can you teach me about XYZ. I say, no, but I know someone who will. That's the power of connection, that I know someone I can point them to." About the dynamics of the festival, Cebuhar says, "There's a great deal of respect here. It's just good energy. I think that this one day a year ... you're going to see, yeah, this can be my community, no demands on you, just come, participate, have conversation, that's the best."

"It's the last thing in the world I ever thought I'd do," said Kirk Thomas, former Archdruid of Ár nDraíocht Féin, speaking of his longtime prison ministry in the state of Washington. "But ADF referred a prison chaplain to me, and eventually the guy convinced me to at least come for a visit. I had no particular training in prison ministry, but they had a need, and this chaplain was determined to serve every one of his inmates, whatever their religion, and one of them was Druid." Over time, Thomas has been invited to join a regional ministerial association and come to be viewed as a valuable resource person for others who have questions about Pagan practice.

Pamela Borawski of Awen Fellowship in central South Carolina had already experienced leadership roles during her earlier years as a Christian. She says, "I started [a private Pagan group called] Circle of Old Souls thinking of it more as a support group because I couldn't find a group that wasn't a secretive coven." Soon after Circle of Old Souls began to flourish, Borawski saw a need for a generalized public Pagan fellowship in her region. Before starting the new Awen Fellowship, she sought intensive training in hypnotherapy, holistic healing and counseling "as a way to heal the world." With her lifelong habit of volunteer support, and working now as a museum docent, she feels strongly about the need for appropriate training.

During her interview, Borawski shared the strategic approach she took to starting Awen Fellowship. She carefully considered what were her mission, vision, and goals. This discernment process underscored her desire to offer herself as a spiritual leader and teacher who would be readily accessible to the public. She has plans to apply for nonprofit status for Awen Fellowship, and is currently building a platform for online teaching. Noting that she had a painful history with her religious past, Borawski said she wanted to avoid the concept of a church or even use of the word "fellowship." But over a year and a half period she continued to feel a calling to found something which did somewhat resemble a church in its organization.

The name Awen Fellowship is a deliberate attempt to reclaim spiritual language, which Borawski feels should not be exclusive to Christians. When I ask if anyone has suggested that the word might be sexist, she adds that she has never thought of the word as gendered. "Fellowship, community, is the one thing that I miss about a church," Borawski muses. "Pagans should be able to have it, too." Borawski envisions Pagan community as embodying the kind of mutual support she feels is a universal human need, defining "fellowship" as a family of likeminded people who support each other.

Christopher Penczak, founder of the Temple of Witchcraft in Salem, New Hampshire, shared how the organization has addressed some needs which can fall through the cracks, especially the development of strong supportive relationships. "I felt like I had no support in terms of mentorship or peership. a lot of what I got [in early years], both good and bad, was rooted in personalities. I saw that we needed to create something with structures to provide accountability for those of us with strong personalities, including myself. Creating peer-to-peer support has been huge, having a network of other ministers, but also students and advanced students and ministers having a space to just talk, explore and share with each other." Penczak points to the many internal groups within the Temple, some for teaching, some for social media, some working groups and some for specific interests, as a way to challenge and engage people, giving them support when they want to go deeper.

Burnout and Conflict

But too many Pagans face compassion fatigue, burnout and conflict in the course of pursuing their visions of ministry. Problems that are common enough in most groups, particularly those which are grassroots and volunteer-led, are exacerbated in the intensely individualistic culture of Pagans. Unclear group member obligations, poor personal boundaries, scarce available resources (including other volunteers), and lack of community codes of behavior have frequently led to discord or, simply, leader exhaustion.

Dana Doerksen discussed her journey of service, which in other groups in the past led to some personal burnout and sometimes even sacrifices of her family obligations. Within the group, she feels there were probably different senses of responsibility, resulting in uneven commitment. "I think a lot of the group felt that it was for them more 'if we can make it,' and for me it was 'no, we have a responsibility to do this.'" She did not perceive any conflict with group members, but increasingly felt that too much work was falling to her. She pointed out the cultural expectations which arose even among Pagans who turned to a group for support. "I think people assumed that we were like Christian ministers, that was our job. Even though we were unpaid and did not have all that time to do things, it was expected that you would call the leader of the group you attended."

Pagano admitted that burnout is an ongoing concern for ministers but made a key distinction. Usually the burnout is not about the priest duties, but about other things in your life. "Priesting is the easiest thing to drop when job and family stress you." His comment reminds us of the task faced by nearly everyone in Pagan ministry, that of finding a balance between spiritual vocation and income-earning. Until a time when Pagans may begin to financially support their ministers, this dilemma deserves serious thought in advance of attempting to build a sustainable ministry constellation.

Although solitary, Pagano is part of a small pan-Pagan peer group that meets from time to time for ritual. In this respect, his group is similar to Christian ministerial breakfast or prayer groups who look for friendship and support outside of the bodies they serve in order to preserve their own boundaries. Others make a practice of training others and intentionally sharing specified leadership duties. Ultimately, one's ministry constellation will be defined at least partially by the limits of time and personal energy one is willing to expend.

Star Bustamonte in Asheville, North Carolina (long known as a haven for witches), expressed frustration with the contradictory attitudes towards commitment that she sees. "My experience with people that say they want to be part of a group, the biggest problem is they don't want to do the work that being part of a group involves, or contribute anything other than just showing up. But 50 percent of the time they're not going to show up even. They all think they want to be part of a group or they have ideas of what they would like to see, but then they don't support those things."

Given the sharp decline in numbers throughout the American Christian world, Pagan reluctance to support community activities may simply reflect a societal wave of change. For arguably two centuries, virtually all American Christians could expect free access to a functioning house of worship and a minister (at least itinerant if not permanent). Even with fewer numbers, from the early eighteenth century on American Jews quickly formed congregations and built synagogues, from Boston to Charleston and Savannah. Most Pagans, even if not raised in a religious household, have lived their entire lives in a society which offered religious community to all, with little or no initial requirement of funds, attendance or work. Pagan spiritual community might easily be taken for granted by some, if they are ambivalent in any way about their own willingness to be engaged.

Bustamonte continued, "I feel like the Pagan community is so at odds and there is such a lack of cohesiveness and unity. People have ideals of what they want, but the reality is I don't see people really putting the energy into creating those things. That's just been my experience. We can all get along for a weekend, but we cannot apparently on a regular basis without our biases coming into play." By this she refers to the popularity of Pagan retreats, festivals and conferences, to which many individuals flock, then returning home afterwards to relative religious anonymity.

Some are unable to avoid breakdown. An anonymous longtime witch confessed to me her own role in her burnout. "I'm done. And here's the thing—It's all my fault. I did this for years and years and years because it's ego. I approached all of this with the knowledge that I could do better and I always believed, and I was taught in the military, that you shut up and stepped up. Pretty much in that order. So that's what I did. My hubris took center stage and I became the ringmaster—I can do this, look at me, aren't I great. The problem came about where nobody was doing things the way they needed to be done, which was perfectly. So I ended up doing it all."

Stressing the importance of self-care, she says, "Life is a lot less complicated [now]. I want to move to the country. I don't want to open a retreat. I don't want other people to come there and have marvelous experiences ... So, I have stepped back." Even following her painful crisis, this leader eventually resumed community activity, and seems to have found a measure of balance. Many do not, however; one Pagan told me that she wished me well in my work but that she would "never, ever, ever again be involved with the Pagan community."

Such finality is regrettable, if understandable. Most who emerge in Pagan ministry or leadership have no formal preparation for the tasks they take on. The initial glow of finding a new religion can easily be followed by premature responsibilities, or unsupported efforts to provide community support. Meanwhile, I maintain that negative outcomes can be avoided or mitigated by training and education, as well as commitment to ethical and transparent processes, by both leaders and group members.

Flexibility, Accessibility, and Social Connections

A few Pagan ministers have demonstrated remarkable success by their longevity. For thirty years Amber K and Azrael Arynn K have been active with their coven, Our Lady of the Woods, which Amber started. During this time they also spun off the Ardantane learning community including purchasing its property in northern New Mexico twenty years ago and building a campus. The coven's motto is "Teaching Wicca, Healing the Earth," so the coven has always been open, even though some individual members are not public about their spirituality. Azrael said that they initially communicated using "all the old-fashioned techniques," like flyers in metaphysical bookstores, word of mouth among friends, and occasional print advertisements in a local Pagan newsletter. As technology came of age, print communications receded, giving way to electronic communication channels, though word of mouth is still highly effective.

Stressing the importance of visibility, Amber pointed out that Ardantane has a growing presence online, and there are frequent articles about it in the local news, including notices of upcoming programs. Like Bustamonte, she points out the influence of the Pagan festival movement, saying, "The more events we have like this that are visible in the community and that are there on a regular basis, the more touchpoints we have where people can connect ... Places where people know they can go and hook up with other Pagans." Amber's and Azrael's "touchpoints" are the nodes in their constellated ministry, allowing individuals to intersect with Ardantane in one or more of several ways.

Everyone I interviewed had some kind of online presence, either as an individual resource, or through an organization website. Cebuhar keeps business cards at hand to give those who may want to contact her later with questions. Most mentioned social media. Wes Isley, an interfaith and Pagan minister who is also part of a North Carolina Vodou house, noted that the main house in New Orleans is very public, but his local meetings are private. Word of mouth is arguably the most common means by which individuals reach Isley,

Cebuhar, and — at least, in earlier years — the other interviewees.

Schreiwer is concerned with communication as a way to preserve his legacy, which is drawn from the lore of the Pennsylvania Dutch. "We are still writing our stuff, we're still oral, but we are trying to get it written down. We share our programs out to the entire community [electronically], and we have some videos out there." He is concerned that many of the last keepers of this lore are quite aged, making his writing, as well as his sharing out of information, vital to its memory and cultural survival. As a leader, Schreiwer encourages people to take on a small job and demonstrate they can assume more responsibility in the future. He says, "I still identify with the cohesion of the community [Mennonite]," underscoring the importance of a diffuse leadership shared by many, rather than a top-down model.

Bustamonte (also director of Mystic South annual conference in Atlanta) told me that the Raven and Crone metaphysical store hosts a welcoming circle once a month, so that seekers and the curious can attend a ritual and meet others, perhaps connecting with a group they will eventually join. The local Mother Grove group (led by Byron Ballard) holds public rituals, and there is a monthly discussion group called Circle Round (also held at Raven and Crone).

But even in a region where Paganism is so popular that for years the Asheville *Citizen-Times* featured a column by Ballard called "The Village Witch," these meetings and groups have fluctuated over the years, prompting periodic change by leaders. And after meeting on Sundays for a while, Borawski found that people did not like giving up their weekends so she changed to a Monday evening. She said, "You have to be flexible. The main thing that doesn't work is not being willing to change." She relies on Facebook and Meetup.com for public announcements, in addition to word of mouth. Lately, she has noticed a subtle shift in the demographics of her participants. When her group first started, most were aged 40s–60s. In the past year and a half she is seeing more young adults, usually in their 20s–30s. Bustamonte, however, asserts that all ages are well-represented among store, meeting and ritual attendees in her region.

Borawski and friends had been holding open full moon ceremonies for more than a year at the time of our interview. She said that many religions and spiritualities are represented by attendees. She welcomes all comers, saying, "We are based in our body and Nature, so it doesn't matter what is our religion." Pondering the possibility that momentum may ebb in the future, she remarks, "If the group went away, I almost feel that I would start another group for the fellowship. I might change tactic, try something new, but I would always want to have a group to come to." The transformational effect of group participation is a key driver for Borawski. "I was solitary for a long time while getting to know myself. I'm introverted, but as far as changing yourself and changing other lives, you have to be around other people. You develop another level by learning to be around people."

Riffe, too, advocates a flexible approach even when teaching and practicing a defined tradition. "I realize that people who are chasing their spirituality — and I say chasing because I don't think any of us ever fully catches it — it's difficult enough, and if you've got kids and a job and a family in the mix and then suddenly you've got this high priestess telling you that you've got to be at ritual at midnight on a Tuesday night, something's going to give." She feels that if spirituality cannot be blended with daily life, it will probably take a back seat to children, home, and work. "So now we have our classes on Saturdays, our full moons are always on the weekend closest to the full moon, and our sabbats are also on the weekend closest to that sabbat."

Another organization which has stood the test of time is Assembly of the Sacred Wheel in Delaware. Ivo Dominguez, co-founder of the Assembly, and a coven priest for nearly four decades, offered a thoughtful discussion of the current Pagan landscape, which he feels grew so fast that many became group leaders who were ill-prepared. As overall expectations diminished, many came to assume that what they were experiencing was all there was to Paganism, leading them to question why they should join a group. He observed that with a limited number of available groups, an individual may join the only thing they can find, discovering later that it is not a good match. In his opinion, small working groups are especially vulnerable to both the advantages and disadvantages of personalities in their groups. One way that the Assembly has strengthened the likelihood of success during the transition in which a new group "hives off" from the original, is to send the standing high priestess off with the new group. In this way, the new high priestess gains her footing in a supportive and familiar culture.

Cebuhar placed emphasis on her Pagan networks, but she has also long been active in her interfaith community, her group having connections with a Sikh group, an independent Catholic church, and a kabbalah group who all meet in the same place. Again, she pointed out the importance of "showing up" in others' space to provide Pagan ritual or instructive classes, or to collaborate for social justice issues. But she also participates in group events in which the varied religious groups determine elements which they can share in a service. She stresses the importance of seeing each other as equals in such settings, with a goal of sharing and growing together. In doing so, she is offering flexibility to those who would meet her in her ministry constellation.

Some scholars have struggled to understand the role of electronic connection in religious communities. Pagan studies researcher Douglas Cowan wrote that there is no virtual community without real-life community, and many close observers of Christian groups have posed related questions.[30] But researchers have found it difficult to separate online connections from real-life. Studies seem to support the idea that online connections can build local communities, in addition to providing support to those unable or unwilling to access a local group.

Needs Served by Ministers and Leaders

What are people looking for when they turn to Pagan ministers? The answers to this question give shape to interviewees' ministry constellations. "The majority are confused; they know they don't believe what they used to and want guidance figuring it out," says Borawski. Most of her students are unsure how to create a practice that reflects their new beliefs, hence the

---

30 Douglas E. Cowan, *Cyberhenge: Modern Pagans on the Internet* (London: Routledge, 2004).

popularity of the Pagan Basics class she teaches. "They come to me saying, 'I'm lost, help me figure out my path,' and next they say, 'I don't know what to do.' I reassure people you don't need the fancy stuff to practice. I help remove the preconceived notions."

Dominguez pointed out the predominance of needs for spiritual support related to family, aging and other life passages. Beaumont, a member of Assembly of the Sacred Wheel, finds that people are looking for someone to talk to before making life decisions. She also sees this when she is with people in the hospital during a crisis. She feels that she will continue her hospital chaplaincy, and add an end-of-life focus to her work with the larger community.

Andersen finds that many come to her for pastoral counseling, Unitarians seeking practical advice, Pagans often asking for esoteric guidance. She says people at their lowest point will call her when they can't see a way forward, relying on her position as a Unitarian Universalist minister. In her role as priestess to her witchcraft group, Andersen is more likely to hear people say, "I think the goddess is talking to me and I'm not sure how to respond."

Noting her own tendency to be an introvert, Cebuhar appreciates that the act of entering a new space or group can be daunting. She is willing to welcome people at the door and help them get over the hump of facing a new environment. She respects their boundaries, but also encourages them to try out something new. "I like to see people grow beyond their own limitations. Connecting with other people is just an expression of my Paganism, my belief in the power of interconnection with everything, with everyone, whether you agree with me or not."

Dominguez finds that people are initially drawn to group membership by a desire for education and ritual participation, and perhaps the opportunity to have a spiritual mentor. Beaumont echoes this idea, saying, "I notice that I sometimes serve in mentoring functions. I get asked questions—I'm the one who can give clear explanations, so people ask me." She pointed out that there are several leadership roles, e.g., ritual leader, mentor, and coven leader, declaring, "I have the first two [talents] but no way I'd have the administrative talent to run a coven." This kind of role clarification no doubt contributes to Beaumont's maintaining balance in her life.

For all of her involvement over the years in public activities, Bustamonte says she is "primarily a solitary," who also wanted the socialization of public groups and events. Insisting that she is capable of doing her own serious ritual and magic alone, she sees group ritual as the opportunity to focus on a specific objective. She feels that when she looks for outside support, she is mainly looking for opinion and advice before acting on her own, saying, "You need that feedback [from others]." Bustamonte does express concern that members of the Pagan community are often at odds, causing erosion to the community. Still when it comes to the need for ministry as evidenced by sheer numbers, she declares, "Every day, I'm telling you ... I have never seen so many witches in my life. It is a steady stream ..."

Thomas feels that he helps provide validation to people who are damaged by their former religion, or have no religious background, and perhaps have had a mystical experience they need to process. He also is a dedicated ritualist. "I made an oath to myself and the gods that whatever my [ritual] commitment was, I would perform the ritual whether anyone shows up or not, do the rite fully robed, full-voice, because I'm doing it for the gods. He advises those who want to lead and minister, You must be prepared for nobody to care. Just decide that this is what you are going to do, and do it. But be consistent—that is so important, so people can count on it, that is critical."

What We Can Anticipate

Asked what Pagan or other spiritual leadership will look like in a decade, Doerksen reflected on her time as a member of the Cherry Hill Seminary Board of Directors. "If you had asked me before I got on the CHS board I would have said we would have more trained people and people would be clamoring to get trained to help and be more useful. And then they didn't come. We still have a lot of folks who really fear large organizations or any power structures that would stem what they are doing." Having voiced her disappointment, Doerksen continues on a more hopeful note, "But a lot of the younger folks I've met in their 20s and 30s, they seem to want more training and experience." With this comment, she both questions whether Pagans can support and sustain reliable resources, and she affirms the desire of successive (younger) generations to serve.

Advising that future survival will require recognizing the transitions which are occurring in modern spiritual communities, Beaumont voiced her concerns for generational transmission of spiritual values. "Organizations that have seen themselves as community leaders are going to have to get into the 21st century. My Unitarian Universalist congregation—I see we have this beautiful old building, and a beautiful long tradition, but our young people come and listen with one ear while they text with another."

Even as she volunteers her chaplain support at a bricks-and-mortar facility Beaumont recognizes that adaptability is vital to the survival of spiritual groups. "The community support that thirty years ago we looked for face-to-face, now comes from the internet. I think face-to-face worship will not go away but I think it's going to have to shift and change, and if it doesn't it will have to focus on its own livelihood and become less effective."

Like Dominguez and Borawski, Amber K noted that the two most important things Ardantane offers are learning in the area of nature spirituality and, simply, community. She said, "Those needs overlap but they are not identical." While Ardantane began as a Wiccan seminary, it broadened its emphasis over time, first to Pagan studies in general, and then as a resource to anyone who holds the earth sacred. They have visitors and participants who are not Pagan, but who "care about the earth and the planet," a value Amber and Azrael view as central and unifying.

After years of cultivating her own newfound Paganism, Borawski determined to live her religion more openly. "We are stepping out into the light more," she says, "We don't have to be so hidden. The world is changing and people are changing. This is enabling us to speak our authentic truth and not be afraid." These societal changes encourage her to consider future classes and retreats that could be made possible with acquisition of property and a building. "With a building, we could have something for children. With more young adults we are seeing more children. My ministry in the future will incorporate families, not just women." Riffe also believes it important to serve families: "Our full moons are family friendly—you got kids, bring them along. I'm supposed to be their spiritual leader, I need to make sure those kids know how to behave in circle, too, and start to understand what we are about."

Thomas had this advice, "Patience and kindness are essential. If you are a basically an impatient person maybe you don't want to take this role. You have to know how to do active listening." He has trained and practiced ritual skills for many years in order to perform ritual which will move both the gods and participants. "As Pagans we deal with mystical concepts and experiences. You need to be comfortable with your own trancework abilities, not just to teach it, but to experience it fully so you can have at least an echo of it when you are leading a ritual. I feel that a strong basis in trance and journeying is essential. It also helps to have some pastoral counseling experience, which Cherry Hill Seminary teaches," said Thomas, referring to his past service as board chair for the Seminary. "People are going to have problems and they are going to come to you. You have got to help people through their grieving, for example. For prison work, you can do this in the group because the others want to help the person who has just lost their mother and couldn't be there. A little healing work is good to know how to do [like reiki]. We can't all be psychologists but we need to know a bit, and have a good list of referral resources."

Each of these leaders expressed to me their own style of compassion for those they serve. Each has negotiated the boundaries of ministry as they identified the two sides of the proverbial coin of vocation: what they are compelled to offer, and what others seek. Borawski shared about one member of her circle whose story is meaningful to her. "I've seen her become a more sovereign being; her husband and her children come to my groups now. I remember how lost she was when she came and how she talked about herself. That's all I want, if I can take all the hardship and pain from my past and use it for someone else so they change, that's my goal. I want people to become more resilient, find their connection to the divine, whatever that may be, and become sovereign in their own life."

Chapter 5

Moving Into The Future

From red ochre in Mesolithic burials to Easter Sunday Mass in Saint Peter's Square, spirituality weaves its way through all of our known human existence. Even recent atheist groups have formed "churches" and held regular community services, complete with bands, singing, silent contemplation, and discussion of ethical dilemmas. Pagan variety seems to straddle several of these worlds, at times engaging in simple animistic gestures like pouring a libation on the land, other times holding formal rituals full of allegory and devotion, and still others, communal drumming and singing the night away before welcoming the sun at dawn. Notwithstanding the inevitable precessions of time and culture, spirituality appears to be a permanent warp on humanity's loom, the constant which underlies whatever color weft we pass across its threads.

How do we honor and support this subtle process by which humans make meaning out of their existence? We have entered a time when we must relinquish our tendency to apply theory and structure from the outside to the internal phenomenon of spirituality. This new time requires the very ethos that is held dear by most Pagans, that of intuitive exploration, listening to the heart, flexing our imagination. If we live in synchronicity with our natural surroundings we already possess a creative adaptability. Awareness of our connectedness with all life can show us the stars in the ministry constellation we inhabit. Careful observation gives us the clues to what our communities need, as well as what methods may best work to connect a community into its own unique constellation.

Discerning Your Constellation

Discernment is about perceiving and understanding that which is obscure. If you are like most of the leaders I spoke to, you did not intend to make for yourself a leadership role. More likely, you found yourself showing up when there was an event, volunteering to take on a task, teaching a class when you found some interested in what you had to say, and then leading ceremony because you and some others wanted to do that together. Before long, you realized that people were turning to you to organize, lead, teach, and advise, whether you were prepared or not. Stumbling into a spiritual leadership path is common among Pagans, another way we are different from mainstream religions' straightforward seminary and subsequent placement with a congregation.

Stepping into a task, while admirable, is doing the obvious. Searching for the obscure, the elusive knowledge of your life's vision, requires the hard work of discernment, a combination of practical thinking, meditation and prayerful reflection, and intuitive comprehension. Discernment takes time, it takes patience, and it requires a commitment to following through whatever is needed in the process. For each of us, it is a different process, but yours will probably include patient personal examination, consulting with others whom you respect, and sharing your work at some point with a mentor with whom you can be honest and from whom you can accept honest feedback.

Whether you got here unwittingly or after careful planning, you can now do a sort of inventory to discern the outlines of your ministry constellation. In some ways, this is a kind of strategic planning process, involving a wide look around you, as well as a looking within for a self-assessment. This section is best approached in a manner not unlike your initial dedication to your tradition. After reading over the rest of the chapter, I suggest you set aside a day, or several hours over more than one day, to perform your preferred devotion at your altar, spend time in meditation, and ask any deity or deities to whom you are dedicated to guide your planning and assessments.

You will want to start a notebook or a computer document to which you can return over the days and weeks after you begin your discernment process. Use it to write your responses to the questions below, but also use it to journal your thoughts along the way. If you are fond of images and colors, make them part of this, too. You might have a graphic, or run across an image that you want to paste into your online document, or simply want to doodle in a hard copy. Don't forget to include music or ambient sound, and scent; Pagans know these are time-proven ways to stimulate parts of your brain that you want involved in your discernment work. Give yourself time during this period to come back to things on a subsequent day, to reread what you have written, to even start over if that's what you feel you should do. When you are ready, begin.

Asking Yourself the Hard Questions

A. What is it I'm doing or want to do?

How did I get into doing this?
Why do I want to do this?
Who is already doing it with me?
How did we meet or find each other?
Who else is doing the same thing or something similar?
What would I be doing differently?
Who would do it if I did not?
What are my core values?
How am I suited for this work?

B. How am I not suited?
Rank each of these factors on a scale, from "well-suited" to "need help or improvement."
What are my past experiences with people and groups?
What worked? What went wrong?
What did I like and what do I regret?
What do I do when I am stressed?
What do I do when I have a conflict with someone else?
What is my support network?

C. Get specific about what I want to do (from A above)
Pick the main three ways I want to provide support.
For each of them, write down who will want to receive that service, what they will want to get out of it and how they will know I'm available.
How will I know if it's working? How will I evaluate effectiveness?
What will I do if more people respond than I can handle?
What will I do if no one responds?

How will I move on or retire when I am ready to do something else?

D. What kind of education and training have I had that would prepare me?
What kind of training should I seek out now?
Who else is already involved, or might be if asked, and what can they provide?
Write about my environmental scans (see below)
Who are my allies and potential partners?
What do I need to do next?

Environmental Scan for a Place-based Ministry

Step One: Start with an assessment of your own vicinity. If you feel compelled to serve Pagans and others in a particular city or region, have you really gotten to know that community? By this, I mean not just individuals or your Pagan group. Do you know the neighborhoods and town and region that you live in? What confronts the people in your part of the world? That includes jobs, the local economy, the current political climate, pressing issues like homelessness, the state of your public infrastructure, voting rights, schools, impact of weather and other disasters, civil rights, and religious congregations. These are the matters that shape everyday life.

A first concern is for *practical needs*. Do a significant number of people in your group work second jobs, or third shift or weekends, and so need meetings that accommodate their schedule? Are they families with children who need minding during meetings, or with elderly parents who require respite care in order for them to get away for a circle? If you want to have a physical meeting, will most locals have transportation to that location? If you want to rent a space, will your attendees be in a position to share the cost? Are you prepared for those with mobility challenges, mental health conditions, those who are deaf or visually impaired, or who do not speak your language? Too often, most of us think of these things a bit late, after someone in a wheelchair responds to our public invitation to a bonfire and drumming.

You can determine these needs through observation over time at existing events, or you can actually survey people that you know, or those who respond to a questionnaire you share around, either in person or online. Remember that you may be probing areas that are sensitive for some, so be respectful and treat responses with discretion. Addressing any needs that come up in your survey, whether informal or systematic requires the next step of your environmental scan.

Step Two: The second concern is about *linking needs with resources*. A competent minister is well-acquainted with the resources in her community. Who offers respite care, where can someone go for counseling, mental health treatment, a divorce attorney, a wheelchair, or to find a babysitter? While these may seem like the personal concerns of the individual or family, these things come up in nearly every group. You need to know where to take or send a woman fleeing domestic violence, and how to reach a social worker if you learn that a child is being neglected. More about this in the section on education and training, but for now, we are still focused on getting a good scan of your locale.

Step Three: Who are *your allies*? Allies can be everyone from a coven-mate, to a local interfaith group, a co-activist in causes you've supported, past teachers and mentors, or even family members, or local, open-minded leaders from other religions. Contrary to often-voiced Pagan assumptions, the rest of the religious groups out there have little to no interest in conflict with us. In fact, many of them are curious about Paganism, wanting to know more about our nature-centered and nature-loving spirituality. The climate crisis has prompted more than a few religious bodies and denominations to take a hard look at how they can better coexist with the rest of creation. Some people are already aware that Paganism provides perspective by which they can better integrate their own religion with an earth-awareness. Other religious allies include people from those faiths which continue to endure true persecution, most notably Jews and Muslims. These are people who both need your support and who are more likely to support you when it comes to challenges to your religious freedom and separation of church and state.

    The best way to locate your religious and social justice allies is to get out in your community and meet them. Attend their services as a courteous guest, go to meetings of the Council on American Islamic Relations (CAIR), the Anti-Defamation League (ADL), Americans United for Separation of Church and State (AU), and anything else you find in your backyard. You don't have to sign on the dotted line, or even agree with everything being said, to find some common ground for collaboration. The same is true with local food banks, homeless shelters, wildlife rescue groups and more. Pagans don't need to start up new Pagan-exclusive human services; we can get involved and have meaningful impact where someone else has already done the hard work of inventing the proverbial wheel. Demonstrating commitment to a good cause while being out of the broom closet builds a positive reputation for Pagans in your community.

I also recommend looking out for opportunities to build individual friendships with key allies. If you meet the faiths representative on the staff of the victim services agency and the two of you seem to click, invite him to join you at the Waffle House on the way to work so you can better coordinate the good work each of you is doing. If you sense that you have a lot to learn from a retired activist with a long history in your town, look for the chance to ask if you might spend some time with her now and then. Our elders are all around, and they understand the importance of mentoring new leadership.

Environmental Scan for a Virtual Ministry

When writing about internet use among Heathens, Pagan studies scholar Jennifer Snook observes, "Today *community* can mean everything or nothing; it is whatever members make it."[31] Virtual connections have shown that a group can be, as she puts it, spaceless, and fully integrated with so-called real life, such that neither online nor offline are seen as separate worlds. More than three-fourths of Pagans may be solitary, but nearly all are connected electronically.

How do you assess the need and resources for a virtual ministry? When doing the place-based environmental scan, you will probably find that some

---

31 Jennifer Snook, *American Heathens: The Politics of Identity in a Pagan Religious Movement* (Philadelphia: Temple University Press, 2015), 60.

who cannot access place-based events like rituals and workshops are better served with online connections. In that case, you will want to know if they have a computer or smartphone, reliable internet access, video and audio capability on their device, and when they are most likely to go online. Do they only wish to privately access written information and videos? Do they want to be part of written discussion threads, or part of real-time conversation and ritual? Are they concerned about privacy when participating or accessing such information? If you plan to run a social media platform or web-based meetings, do you have a privacy policy about safeguarding people's contact information and images?

If you will mostly connect to others remotely, are you willing to be available on occasion for face-to face meetings? Are you able and willing to travel to be with those individuals in special settings, such as a retreat, or at a conference in another region, or if they invite you to come teach their group for a weekend? If you want to allow people who have connected with you electronically to visit you in your home, or gather for home meetings, first consider the privacy and safety of yourself and those sharing your household. Have a conversation with them and reach agreement about how often and for how long such meetings take place, who can come into your home, and what to do if someone turns out to make others uneasy.

Even when providing spiritual support with a primarily electronic locus, you will probably find that you have many of the same needs as a place-based ministry, except that you might find yourself wondering, for example, how to quickly connect someone contemplating suicide with the emergency services where they live. A national resources and hotlines list is essential; a good one is found on the website for Cherry Hill Seminary, under News and Resources, called Emergency Resources. Although the efficacy of online groups is still being debated, many Pagans participate in such groups, and for some, that is their only option for group participation, or even one-on-one connection. Researchers have found that online spiritual participation does not detract from a person's spiritual or religious practice, and even enhances their other activities. Some Pagan leaders have already employed this method of outreach for several years; a constellated ministry should consider making such a group or groups available. The Pagan Engagement survey found that even among solitaries, a significant number of people want to be part of some kind of group. An online group is a point of entry that can lead to other resources in your ministry constellation, if a participant wishes to pursue them.

The Nodes in Your Constellation

You are probably bursting with ideas if you have applied yourself rigorously to your personal discernment and environmental scans. Borrowing again from classic strategic planning process, the next step is for you to line up your existing activities or programs, your assets, if you will, alongside the challenges you face and gaps you want to fill. Take a hard look at what is possible, what is realistic, what is a dream, and what may not be such a good idea. Sift out the ways that you want to create your supportive Pagan ministry. If you are on your own, I suggest that you narrow it down to what you can count on one hand. These strategies become the nodes or points of light in your ministry constellation. Examples may include events such as these:

- Monthly public full moon ceremony.
- Teaching or book group
- Annual retreat, festival, concert or workshop
- Availability for individual pastoral counseling
- Video talks posted online
- Weekly group volunteer activity (like sorting recyclables, filling homeless supply kits, etc.)
- Real-time online discussion, ceremony, presentation
- Website with resources and information
- Social media regular presence
- Monthly drumming or craft meet
- Storytelling circle
- Ritual with yoga or tai chi or circle dances
- Families with children gathering

What is your most important program, the one to which you are committed above all others? It may be something you are already doing, something by which you are already known. This is the brightest star in your constellation and should always receive your closest attention. When scanning the night sky, the first thing a stargazer may notice are the three stars in the belt of Orion. Those three will then lead the amateur astronomer to see the feet, the sword, and maybe even the head of Medusa that Orion holds. Or maybe those first stars are beauty enough to feed that person's soul. Your brightest star may or may not connect an individual to other programs in your ministry constellation, but it leads the way.

Following identification of your flagship program, you will probably see quickly how the connections fall into place. At this point you might choose some small objects (like pebbles, shells or large beads) to represent your programs. Lay them out where you can arrange and rearrange them as you consider where they belong in your plan.

Maybe you've had a drumming group for a few years; you've made no secret of your spirituality, and close most sessions with a brief inspirational reading. Several attendees have stayed after to ask you about what you read, inquiring about how they can learn more. For a while now, a couple of the regulars have come to you for advice about personal and family problems. This spring, the group wants to hold a community ceremony at a park by the river to celebrate the season. Clearly, you already have at least four points glowing: the drumming group, pastoral counseling, public group ceremony, and the glimmerings of interest in a class or book study.

A group of nodes do not a hearth or coven make (though they could). It's very likely that a number of your folks have never even heard the term Pagan, or any other related practice, but have come to trust you and feel simpatico with others they meet in your company. The two who contact you once in a while for personal support may not have the slightest interest in reading a witchy book, but they like talking about spirituality with you. And there may be many more friends, family members of the drumming group, and people who are already committed to other groups, who would enjoy participating in a community ceremony in the spring. If you are watching numbers, you quickly see that there is a flux and regular flow among these activities. Some of the additional stars in your constellation are brighter, some dimmer, but the connections among them give shape to the work you feel compelled to do.

And what are the connections? In this sample situation, most people can trace their access to you back to your drumming circle. Your success with the circle indicates that you have a well-established way of circulating information about it. If you want to turn up the brightness in one of the other stars, you might put out information at each drum circle: small printed cards offering your pastoral counseling services, or flyers inviting people to volunteer for the spring ceremony. Or you only give the pastoral counseling cards to people privately, or just to those who ask or who you've helped before. Is there anyone in the group who is already attending a study group elsewhere? Chat with them about what's available, what made them go there, and whether there is interest in what you want to study. You may want to go take the same class with them (part of your environmental scan) before deciding whether to offer a topic, or whether to ask someone you trust to collaborate with you. You could also decide that this other provider is doing a great job that you do not need to duplicate, and they go into your stash of resources to which you can refer people drawn to your constellation.

The process of identifying and building these connections will probably lead you to set up your own ministry website or social media channel to facilitate easy communication. These can easily become a program of their own, depending on how much content you want to put out through them. Or they can simply be a place for people to find you, access your programs, and connect with each other. It should go without saying that your constellation need not be all things to all people. As your community ministry develops, you will know when to add or remove strategies, when to pass on something to another capable leader, and when to make a program one that is a partnership or collaboration among leaders.

The above scenario is very simple, the activities and connections straightforward and common enough these days. What is new is that you are both participating in and accommodating a fluid community. You are not attempting to control what you cannot, but you are giving individuals a number of ways to engage, participate, and derive spiritual support. A mature spiritual leader will also encourage individuals to explore other resources and groups outside of her constellation, not hoarding those in her group. In the constellated ministry model, neither a minister, nor a location, is the focus; rather, the focus is the complex of activities and the people moving into and out of them. This better reflects the rapid changes that characterize our post-industrial contemporary society. It is also a healthy way to nurture humans' inherent natural spiritual creativity.

Starting from Scratch

One of the leaders I interviewed pointed out that she had done "this work" all her life, beginning with her childhood church. She said that after becoming Pagan she spent years as a solitary, processing her past and becoming grounded in her new spiritual identity. In time, however, she began to seek fellowship with others. Eventually, this led to her holding a regular public full moon ceremony, teaching classes at a local occult store, and offering her healing services. She made a point of explaining that she only did this after spending considerable time determining her personal ministry vision, goals and mission, much like a nonprofit creates its strategic plan. This rootedness in meaning gives her a strong, yet peaceful, demeanor that reassures those who come to her. She is also clear that she and other leaders must remain flexible, willing to change what they are doing, or how, if it becomes obvious that something is no longer working.

This story underscores the importance of building one's spiritual foundation. Although you will find that your service to others is a constant journey of learning, you owe it to yourself and others to start by deepening your own personal practice and exploring your theology of service, that is, why are you doing this? You will still encounter many questions, and perhaps some dark nights of the soul, along the way, but with preparation you will be better able to navigate those times.

Recently I read some articles by an organizational consultant, Susan Beaumont, who specializes in working with churches facing change. Beaumont has written a book, *How to Lead When You Don't Know Where You're Going*.[32] That title would seem to put it right out there—after doing your personal discernment and environmental scan, you may be very clear about stepping forward, but not as clear about your plan. Beaumont notes the success she has had with her congregational clients by setting up listening circles and using a technique called appreciative inquiry to find out as much as she can from the people in a particular religious

---

32 Beaumont, Susan. *How to Lead When You Don't Know Where You're Going: Leading in a Liminal Season* (Lanham, Md.: Rowman & Littlefield, 2019).

community. In *How to Lead When You Don't Know Where You're Going,* she talks about the importance of accepting that sometimes we must wait patiently in liminal space until the right moment comes for action, action based on intentional group discernment. Maybe you have your own listening circle in the form of your spiritual group, or a select group of allies and advisors, who will meet with you from time to time. Think of them as midwives as you approach your time of giving birth.

On the other hand, opportunity may nudge you to join the Fool of the tarot in stepping off the cliff towards a new adventure. If you have done that and are still on your feet, congratulations! But if you are still in liminal space, be grateful for the chance to listen, watch and plan. This foundation can give you confidence down the road when you are challenged by situations and questions you could not have foreseen at the beginning.

Moving Towards Excellence

The Pagan Engagement and Spiritual Support Survey provided valuable data about what Pagans in the United States value in their spiritual practice, what they want by way of spiritual support or group affiliation, and what has gone wrong for them. If we take the survey results at face value, here are the key findings in summary.

People most value about their groups —

- Opportunity to learn and grow
- Social bonds formed with others who share their spirituality.

People choose to be solitary because of —

- Preference for autonomy;

- Too much time involved
- Group dysfunction and poor leadership.

The things valued are elements found desirable by people almost universally, not just in religious settings but in all kinds of groups. The reasons for solitary practice are similarly issues we might anticipate. I take this input as clear direction for how Pagan ministers can increase their odds of success in their communities. We should invest in what people value by supporting the ways that best help them achieve their goals. And we must support and protect healthy social bonds by providing opportunities for group bonding, and by protecting the social-emotional dynamics of the group. Let's examine each of these factors individually.

Opportunity to Learn and Grow

People want to learn and grow and, according to the survey, they feel this happens in community. This suggests the importance of teaching, mentoring, book groups, online topical discussion, and the ability to access additional resources. Find out what the people drawn to your constellation want to learn about. If you are not sure, invite several people to meet you for coffee or a brew and get them talking. If you are not a skilled, knowledgeable teacher, locate individuals who are and invite them to present to your group. Add links to reputable articles and online classes to your online presences. When you present or teach, allow ample time for questions, discussion and group interaction, for multidirectional learning among group members, not just a top-down flow of static information. Encourage people to see their whole life as a chance for learning and growth, to pay attention to the flow of their lives, and be patient with the pace they need.

In the time when the coronavirus pandemic permeated every aspect of our lives, many who would previously have refused to consider online rituals, meetings and teaching came to embrace virtual space. If you are making the digital plunge, don't stop with simply signing up for a meeting application like Zoom. Here are my best suggestions for making these occasions memorable for the content (and not for the tech snafus).

- Watch some video tutorials about effective online meeting management. There are some useful features, like co-hosting, sharing your screen, whiteboards and breakout rooms, which are easy to manage and give you some flexibility in approach.
- Get a microphone headset that plugs into your computer (not wireless). Ask your guests to do the same. Mute people when they are not speaking.
- Practice with a friend before actually holding something online. Have a backup plan for what to do when things go wrong.
- Don't spend too much time fussing with tech. People don't join your events just to hear you discuss computer problems and delay getting started.
- Smile, be friendly, treat participants with the same warmth you would if they were at an in-person event. The message of your ritual or workshop will have more meaning if you make the effort to involve all present, if not with a role, then at least with your welcome.

Building Community Social Bonds

Even among survey respondents who are solitary, many indicated that they would like to be part of a group if there were one accessible and appropriate for them. Nearly everyone who responded wrote that they attend open circles, workshops, conferences and festivals at least some of the time and value the friendships that result. Awen Fellowship's Pamela Borawski told me that fellowship, as she called it, is so important to her that if her current groups were to wind down, she would start something else so that likeminded people could come together. She told me, "I was solitary for a long time while getting to know myself ... but as far as changing [personal change] and changing other lives [ministry] you have to be around other people. You develop another level by learning to be around people." Your constellation will probably benefit by offering some occasions for people to come together, in person, if possible, or at least virtually, in real time.

Again, pandemic constraints showed us that more people are able and willing to join an online event than we may have expected. Curiosity and accessibility can overcome the obstacles of travel and physical challenges that prevent many from in-person participation. Some who are shy in a group may decide to try out attending an online event, knowing they can simply turn off their camera or even quietly leave. But whether online or on-site, building a community requires consistency and continuity. When people know they can count on a regular gathering, they are more likely to develop a habit of showing up. If you erratically schedule, abruptly reschedule or cancel, and fail to communicate events well in advance, you are signaling to participants that their needs and time are not important to you.

Preference for Autonomy and Concerns About Time Commitment

A fair amount of nuance emerged from survey comments written by solitaries. Some had not found a group which reflected their own beliefs or practice, saying it was easier to connect to the sacred when alone, or that they simply preferred individual autonomy. About the same number found group activities to be inconvenient, too time-consuming, or otherwise overly demanding.

I would add that people move in and out of seasons in their lives; a meeting that is inconvenient while caring for a terminally ill spouse may become a highly desired place for healing in the year following the spouse's death. Changes in jobs, relationships, start of school in the fall, and family finances — all of these and more can impact a person's ability and willingness to become involved with any new commitment. This is another reason that overlapping and interactive ministry constellations, including a variety of channels for access, can be more effective, addressing the needs of both group members and those who choose to be solitary.

Group Dysfunction and Poor Leadership

The number of survey participants citing poor leadership, group dysfunction, and even abuse as reasons to avoid group activities was nothing short of disconcerting. Issues most commonly raised were about internal group power struggles, inability to resolve differences, lack of direction, manipulation, and a shallow approach to spirituality and practice.

People who have a negative past experience with Pagans will quickly learn whether or not you are able to nurture and protect a safe space. Failing to care for the well-being of the group, allowing one or two individuals to dominate conversation, dismissal or disregard of damaging gossip—all of these things strongly signal that you value something other than helping people heal, learn and grow. Much has been written about why leaders should be trained and mentored; this book does not attempt to reproduce the wealth of available leadership development resources. Nearly anyone with a sincere desire to serve others should be able to access at least a good book from the library, if not a class or program online, or at the local library or any number of local agencies and organizations.

Trolls and Antagonists

We might think of so-called trolls, people who post inflammatory remarks for the sake of starting arguments in online groups, as something which came into its own with internet access. But what church consultant Kenneth Haugk[33] calls "antagonists" have probably always been around. Whenever disagreements and conflict become the characteristic of an individual's relationship with a group, there are the makings of group dysfunction or even dissolution. Some find their way to feel empowered is by damaging others and attempting to control the group in an unhealthy

---

33 Kenneth C. Haugk, *Antagonists in the Church: How to Identify and Deal with Destructive Conflict* (Minneapolis: Augsburg, 1988).

way. Often we in leadership enable this process in the beginning, thinking that we are being inclusive, that we are listening and caring about the concerns of such a person. Before we know it, factions are lining up on various sides, and the same person who seemed like a friend has begun to lead opposition to what had been working before they came on the scene.

Good leadership training can help groups and their leaders to recognize dysfunctional behavior and respond appropriately. Sometimes that response looks harsh, like (as in a worst-case) an expulsion from the group or public warning to the spiritual community. It bears repeating that group leaders have a responsibility to protect the health of the group as a whole. The terms "group dysfunction" and "poor leadership" are somewhat general.

The previous key factors were closely followed by some other important needs which deserve their own attention here. Some of the recommendations in the next few sections can help a group be in a stronger position to avoid serious problems.

Better Understanding and Accommodation of Those with Disabilities

Accommodation of different physical, mental and emotional abilities should be second nature to us all, years after the Americans with Disabilities Act, the European Accessibility Act, and Canadian Human Rights Act became law. Behavioral standards and cultural understanding can be a little trickier; good training from valid, competent individuals is well worth the time and money your group puts into it. It's no longer acceptable to hold events in locations which prohibit participation because they are not wheelchair-accessible, for example. If your group loves to hike to a remote location for a ritual, that's great, but are there some you are leaving out because they are unsteady on their feet, or need a toilet close by? These are things you should ask participants to talk with you and each other about, determining solutions together.

Much as I love sage and incense, my group was very reserved about their indoor use during the years that we had a member with severe asthma. Recently, she passed away during a sudden asthma attack. We would have missed years of her wise counsel and friendship had we not accommodated her special health need. I have also experienced the disruption to group meetings by attendees with mental disorders. By learning how to respond to them appropriately we were able to continue to include them. Their disability did not have to exclude their attendance, but it also did not have to negatively impact the experience of the overall group. Being prepared for those with such needs is the responsibility of a good spiritual leader or minister. These are but a few examples; your group may find itself learning American Sign Language together, installing better lighting in your meeting places, or ride-sharing for those who cannot drive. Whatever you face, let compassion for others and the well-being of all you lead be your guide.

Respectful Recognition of Cultural Differences

Culture includes numerous characteristics, ethnicity and natal origin being only the two most obvious. Looking at devotional styles, some come to Paganism eager to shed the somber worship experience of their childhood, ready to "whoop it up" around a fire, explore trancelike states, and enter fully into an exuberant, celebratory mode of ritual. Then there are others who had enough of that approach in the past and are seeking a more serene mysticism. Some need physical activity and loud drumming, singing or chanting to raise and release energy. Others need a gentle, sensitive container for ritual, a place in which they can meet the numinous without distraction. Respectful consideration of cultural differences do not have to displace your personal style and preferences, for example, if you are leading rituals. But it is wise to discuss with your group what is meaningful to them, working together to create a shared ritual culture.

This would also be the time to talk about what is appropriate to borrow from various cultures. Cultural appropriation has become a hot topic in the past decade as we come to understand the hurt we can cause others when we carelessly adopt a practice or the attire of a culture with which we have no authentic connection. Native Americans and other Indigenous peoples, particularly in North America, are especially sensitive to how non-Natives have used their cultural elements to gain financial profit. Before you call on White Buffalo Calf Woman, ponder your own relationship to and knowledge of her origins and what she meant to the people who first recognized her.

AORTA (see Resources) has an excellent handout about cultural appropriation that you can use as a discussion guide with others. It includes talking points like these.

- Does the source group or culture have a history of exploitation, slavery, or genocide? If so, there is

already a social power dynamic at play regarding the use of their culture.
- Are you buying this directly from the community? Does your participation in it benefit the community?
- Is the source's significance filling a hunger (for "sacredness," for "meaning")? Is this facilitating or participating in "shopping" from cultures?
- Is it taking just a piece of an image, custom, or practice out of context?[34]

Pagans often feel a particular draw to cultures which are new to them. Stepping into a different worldview can be an immeasurably valuable practice, opening fresh insights and offering practices which nourish our souls. If it is a living culture from which you gain inspiration, connect with the community to learn directly, in the process finding out what is acceptable to emulate, borrow or adapt. If the culture is ancient, you probably need not be concerned about power dynamics or inappropriate financial profit. Even so, the more you learn about the source culture which inspires you, the more meaning you will find in it.

Accountable Standard Business Practices

Distilling the essence of all these factors reveals them to be extensions of our concern for treating each other with compassion. Whether a threefold law, a golden rule, the Hippocratic Oath, or any other code of behavior, most of us can agree that we should treat others as we would like to be treated. The same goes for

---

[34] AORTA, https://aorta.coop/portfolio_page/cultural-appropriation/.

financial and organizational accountability. Get advice from someone with a good track record, who can teach you the right way to keep records, make decisions, and be transparent. Transparency and record-keeping are not so difficult, but they too often destroy trust and divide us. Set up a system from the beginning. The Free Management Library (see Resources) offers one of the best free sources of articles and links on every topic imaginable, from bookkeeping, to strategic planning, teams and groups, leadership and fundraising.

Addressing Our Deeper Wounds

Abuse has always been a problem, not unique to any religion, nor even to one gender. It occurs across economic, educational, age and any other difference that exists between humans, and can be found throughout most of our ancient sacred texts. This section does not replace professional training, but the issues are so pervasive that they had to be addressed here. Once upon a time, Pagans did not want to see the inappropriate behavior and outright abuse among us. But we don't just have a responsibility to address abuse. We also have an obligation to use our moral authority as spiritual leaders to create and maintain safe spaces, as well as to model ethical conduct. If we are truly a sex-positive religion, then we must face head-on the need to develop clear standards for ethical and safe groups, with no tolerance of sexual abuse.

Prevention of sexual abuse and domestic violence is easier by far than trying to repair the aftermath. The most important principle of what is called "consent culture" is the irrevocable integrity of the individual and their right to choose whether or not to engage in any sexual behavior, or even to be touched. While the individual may make a unilateral decision about themselves, a true consent culture develops when everyone present possesses the empathy to respectfully seek consent and honor others' boundaries. Christine Hoff Kraemer and Yvonne Aburrow have developed an outstanding web page which is listed in the References section. The site includes model policies, a study guide and links to other resources, all grounded in an understanding of Pagan culture and spiritualities.

Sexual Abuse and Domestic Violence

Lest you assume that sexual abuse and other violence are unlikely ever to affect the people you serve, here are a few statistics to disabuse you of that myth. The numbers below are from a from a 2015 report by the Centers for Disease Control and Prevention and a 2015 report by the U.S. Department of Justice Office of Justice Programs.

- Twenty people are physically abused every minute in the United States.[35]
- One in five women and 2.6 percent of men in the United States have been raped at some point in their lives.[36]

---

[35] Truman, Jennifer and Morgan, Rachel. *Nonfatal Domestic Violence, 2003-2012*, U.S. Department of Justice Office of Justice Programs, April 2014.

[36] S.G. Smith, X. Zhang, K.C. Basile, M.T. Merrick, J. Wang, M. Kresnow, and J. Chen. *The National Intimate Partner and Sexual Violence Survey (NISVS): 2015 Data Brief – Updated Release*. Atlanta National Center for Injury Prevention and Control, Centers for Disease Control and Prevention, 2018.

- More than 81 percent of women were raped for the first time before they were 25 years old.[37]
- Almost 72 percent of male victims of rape were under age 25 the first time; 26 percent of them were under age 10.[38]
- One in seven women and one in eighteen men have been stalking victims.[39]
- One in seven women and one in four men have experienced severe physical violence by an intimate partner (beating, burning, strangling, e.g.).[40]
- Domestic violence accounted for 21 percent of all violent crime from 2003-12.[41]
- 19 percent of domestic violence involves a weapon.[42]

The number of people among us (and many of we ourselves) who carry permanent psychic wounds left by such trauma can be shocking. There is no doubt that far more violence, proportionally, is experienced by people of color, LGBTQ+ individuals, and people who belong to often vilified marginalized groups like people of Native American, Latinx, Middle Eastern, South Asian or other descent. Sadly, crimes against Muslims, Jews and Sikhs have also risen dramatically since September 11, 2001. They all deserve our best efforts at awareness and inclusion.

Keep in mind that trauma hides in unexpected corners of a life. The children who watch their father beat their mother, or one mother beat their other mother;

---

37 Ibid.
38 Ibid.
39 Ibid.
40 Truman and Morgan, *Nonfatal Domestic Violence*.
41 Ibid.
42 Ibid.

the person whose friend calls to say goodbye just before committing suicide; the one who had to be caretaker for the family while growing up with a single alcoholic or addicted parent; the adult who gradually begins to remember and grieve for childhood molestation; the father who lost custody of his children. There are so many ways that humans hurt each other. Part of our responsibility as ministers is caring for those with old wounds, as well as watching for possible signs of ongoing abuse.

Don't Look Away: Recognizing & Responding to Abuse for Non-Professionals is a free download slide show (see Resources) that you can review for yourself and which is also suitable to present to any group. It lists these warning signs of abuse in adults: depression, body image issues, eating disorders, medical problems, stress and anxiety, mental health problems, relationship issues, and sexual difficulties. Abuse of children can be more elusive as they are usually the victims of a family member or friend and may be intimidated or frightened of revealing the abuse, or worse, think that such behavior is normal. *Don't Look Away* gives important steps to take (and not take) if you suspect abuse is happening on your watch. All states require ministers, along with other helping professionals, to contact police or social services immediately if you have credible grounds for suspicion. This may be the most difficult decision you ever make in the course of your ministry, but it may also save a life, or a lifetime of pain. If you look away from the abuse, you have become complicit in perpetuating it.

Addiction and Substance Abuse

An annual survey by the U.S. Substance Abuse and Mental Health Services Administration (SAMHSA) reported that in 2018 nearly 6 percent of Americans age 18 or older suffered from Alcohol Use Disorder (AUD).[43] Addiction to one category of drugs alone, opioids, has caused so many overdose deaths that it is now referred to as an epidemic. Only a small number of people acknowledge addiction issues, and still fewer are successful in their struggle to break free of the habits of addiction. We may assume that at least some alcoholics and addicts are Pagan. Their spouses, family members, friends and coworkers often represent a secondary levels of wounds. Added to the obvious health detriments and damaged self-esteem, peripheral damage from substance abuse can include domestic violence, crime, job loss and more.

Contemporary North American Paganism came of age in the years (1960s forward) that experimentation with drugs became a cultural phenomenon, and so has typically held a broad view of the use of substances which lead to altered states. Such openness can easily lull us into excusing or simply not recognizing the signs of substance abuse in others. Because alcohol and some drugs are socially acceptable and legal misuse can easily be hidden, support or treatment can be avoided, even for years. All individuals who wish to serve their spiritual communities in any way should seek training in recognizing and responding to substance abuse (often called AOD issues, for alcohol and

---

43 Substance Abuse and Mental Health Services Administration (SAMHSA), *2018 National Survey on Drug Use and Health* (NSDUH) (Washington, D.C.: 2018).

other addictions). Most states have an agency dealing with substance abuse, usually with county or regional offices. These are a good place to start when seeking training.

Of course, the first support that comes to mind for most of us is Alcoholics Anonymous (AA) or one of its many spinoffs like Narcotics Anonymous, and the family support groups like AlAnon. The ubiquity of so-called Twelve Steps groups is a tribute to the lasting success of its approach: completely anonymous, run by members with no outside authority, with a system of addicts mentoring other addicts (mentors are called sponsors). The founders of AA wrote its basic principles, the Blue Book, from their own Judeo-Christian frame of reference. While the twelve steps are models of inclusivity, that inclusivity is somewhat dated, and even objectionable for Pagans who are averse to the Abrahamic religious culture.

My advice is twofold. First is to encourage someone to at least try a Twelve-Step meeting for a time. The camaraderie and unconditional support are outstanding. Particularly for someone who has "hit their bottom," as is often said in the recovery community, polite silence during the occasionally offered Lord's Prayer is a small exchange for support by others who understand. Second is to look at one of several Pagan versions of the Twelve-Step programs which are listed in the Resources section of this book.

A word of caution: the general wisdom is that an alcoholic should never drink again. Some people resent this stricture, saying at your cookout, I'm just going to have one, or I've been "clean now for a year." Help that person to remain clean and sober by reminding them that you are supporting them in their new life. Groups which normally include alcohol in their rituals may also wish to consider other ways of honoring their traditions, such as encouraging people to either lift a cup in respect or pour a libation on the ground, or by using water instead of alcohol.

Moral Wounds

Our military members and veterans and members of our law enforcement agencies are subject not only to violence or even death, but to something now being called moral injury. Post-traumatic stress disorder (PTSD) has received much attention the past few decades, but moral injury can be an even more insidious, invisible trauma. In the United States, as in most places around the world, we raise our children to believe that killing and harming others is wrong. But when they go into the armed forces they are then taught the science of killing and harming as a way of ensuring that national policy goals (including the safety of civilians) are protected. These ideas stand in mutual contradiction to each other, causing many service members to endure a crisis of conscience.

To complicate matters, starting with the Vietnam War, many of our veterans came home from often-horrifying experiences to hate and derision erupting in the wake of the peace movement. Soldiers serving in the Middle East have often returned filled with bitterness about the apparent futility of their efforts. Renowned author Edward Tick (see Resources) notes that PTSD must be seen as a disorder of identity itself, compounded by knowing that no one really understands unless they have had the same experience. Until recently, military culture and training have discouraged revealing such internal conflicts and the Veterans Administration has been uneven at best in providing support.

As the United States grinds into year after year of continuous war overseas, plus the fear of a new cold war, growing numbers of people are affected by moral injury. As with other kinds of emotional wounds, many others are affected—family, coworkers, friends and, on sad occasion, strangers who happen to be present when a veteran becomes unhinged. Experts like Tick say that the deeper healing needed by those suffering PTSD and moral injury comes from being in community. Ministers and leaders will encounter more and more of the soul-wounded and should learn more about how to effectively support them.

Crime Victims

Only a few years ago it would not have occurred to any of us that a section in this book would need to address the topic of mass shootings. Nevertheless, as a Red Cross Disaster Spiritual Care volunteer I have found myself deployed to four such incidents, and there were many more to which I might have been sent. Any type of "mass casualty incident" creates a kind of trauma which can hardly be described. Not only the families of the deceased and the survivors suffer, but there are widening circles that impact whole communities. While in Las Vegas after that notorious 2017 tragedy, I learned that people from around the country and many other countries had been present. Of the more than twenty-two thousand at the Route 91 Harvest music festival that night, nearly one thousand were injured, and fifty-nine died. An estimated thirty attendees found themselves in another mass shooting only a year later, and one of those lost his life there (Thousand Oaks, California).

But the physical injuries were only the external evidence of the significant emotional trauma most had acquired (not unlike the impact of unseen military moral wounds). The majority of people present in Vegas were visitors, tourists only in town for the festival. By Monday morning, most had returned home, where I have no doubt others have been affected by the trauma of their returning loved ones. Some of the people I spent time with included paramedics, still shocked by the chaos and blood at emergency rooms, or a hotel executive trying to simultaneously manage his own pain and his responsibility for addressing the cancellation of 80 percent of reservations that immediately came in. Law enforcement, emergency medical responders, hospitals, and health workers were all stretched beyond their limits that night and in the coming days. City, county, state, and federal agencies jostled to work out protocols for their responses, sometimes effectively, sometimes not.

But there are crime victims in every town, throughout the year. In the recent past we have seen the entire nation rise up in anger and grief over police violence which seems directed at people of color. Many of us feel the call of conscience to do something to heal the pain and prevent it from happening again. Efforts to restore justice in wounded communities are usually a long-term commitment, best undertaken in collaboration with community partners. A leader or minister should approach this kind of spiritual support with the understanding that complex multi-layered social issues are likely to challenge them emotionally. The

"Tools For The Journey" section below talks about the importance of building your own supportive allies.

Staying Safe

My friend Peter was part of a church helping one of its members leave an abusive marriage. One Saturday a crew from the church rented a truck, and as they began the task of loading up the woman's furniture, her husband showed up with a gun. Peter was on the front porch when the woman came to the door to see what was going on. He stepped in front of her just in time to see the husband raise his firearm, and he took a bullet to save her life. But Peter was only one of three people shot in that moment. In fact, he is the only one who survived what next became a murder-suicide.

Modern Pagans have typically felt vulnerable to attacks based on their religion, but it turns out this has rarely been the problem that it is for some religious groups. We now live in a society which is most often polarized by ideologies, often having to do with race and social class. Others simply work at a business where a disgruntled employee comes to work and begins shooting indiscriminately. Mother Emanuel church in Charleston, South Carolina, was a target for a white supremacist murderer because it is a historic symbol of blacks' fight for freedom.

Never underestimate the potential for irrational behavior when abuse or ideology is involved. Encourage a report to the police if you are helping a victim because incidents of violence need to be recorded. If you can, find out whether there are firearms in the home, or an arrest history. Without retreating into fearfulness, consider whether you need to take extra precautions about your own household and family. Simple awareness of surroundings, letting a loved one know where you are at all times, and maybe a doorbell security camera, are reassuring in these uncertain times. My hope is that this will never be a problem for you.

Pastoral Counseling and Support

What do Pagans really want from a leader or minister by way of spiritual support? We are an assertively independent bunch, often feisty about our autonomy. Nevertheless, it is the rare individual who does not come to a time in his life when he needs someone to talk to about personal matters, or advice about finding his way spiritually. I asked interview subjects, "Why do seekers come to you?" One person responded very directly, that most come to her feeling confused and unsure of how to move forward with their spiritual questions. This leader observes, "People are hurting, they don't know how to deal with trouble and pain in their lives. I think that's why people go to any kind of church or group in the beginning. They want to know that somebody is there with them."

For those readers who have received professional training to be a licensed social worker, nurse, psychologist, minister or chaplain, you already understand the obligations of helping vocations. For those just now coming into your leadership path, I urge you to put aside your ego or fantasies of being the essential player in others' life paths. A chaplain will be the first to tell you that at least 90 percent of their work is listening—literally. As a minister, you will be there to accompany people on their healing, learning and living journeys. Sometimes you will be walking in front of them, but you should always be looking for a way to go forward side by side. You are performing your work at its best when you are able to slow down or step away and find happiness in watching the person you have mentored run ahead into their own destiny.

Constellated Ministry is written to share my vision of ministry in changing times, to give limited guidance to the average Pagan who finds herself in leadership and ministry, and to give some background to chaplains and others who want to know how to best serve their Pagan clients. If you are in the former category, be aware that there are some activities which are regulated by state licensure, and for good reason. You may not call yourself a counselor unless you have had clinical training and supervised experience. The terms pastoral counseling or holistic counseling are often used so that expectations are clear that you are offering spiritual guidance, not mental health services. If you consider healing to be part of your vocation, be clear that you are not offering medical advice unless you are a doctor. These are not onerous restrictions, but just more ways that we demonstrate honesty which places the well-being of a client above our own gain.

My survey participants said that they turn most often for support to a friend or family member, if they are solitary Pagans, while group members most often turn to a member of their group. Few of either category would go to someone like a mental health professional. And yet any number of Pagans out there work as mental health counselors, hospital or hospice chaplains, psychologists, social workers, and other helping professions. It's probable that a number of them also provide support of some kind to their local Pagan community. But Pagans who decide to serve as chaplains and pursue a traditional seminary education are seldom perceived as a resource to the Pagan community, even if the community is aware of their work with a hospital, the armed forces, or a hospice. I encourage those professionals to let their Pagan communities know that you can be a resource, either for direct services, or to help refer people appropriately, when they need more support than a friend can give. Pagan leaders can best serve others by referring individuals to professional resources when appropriate.

If you do not possess training or credentials in a helping profession, I encourage you to review the training recommendations in the next section. Pastoral education usually teaches leaders appropriate and effective ways to work with the disabled, parents and children, the mentally ill, and other special populations, or refer them to professional resources. Such training has not typically been accessed by Pagans even though these populations are found throughout the Pagan community. Pagan leaders, in particular, should actively seek education, to better provide support to individuals and guidance to Pagan groups.

One solution is for more grassroots leaders to seek additional, if basic, training by qualified professionals in the key areas of ministry: ethics of ministry, family dynamics, mental health and addiction issues, the theology and practice of ritual, leadership and group dynamics, practical aspects of leading small groups and teaching, basics of pastoral counseling and spiritual support, and an overview of Paganisms and our recent history.

Tools for the Journey

Ministry and leadership are arts, but many aspects of ministry involve skills which can be learned and resources that you can and should develop.

Educational and Training Needs

Pagans are beginning to recognize the critical need for development of ministry standards that will result in safe, nurturing groups, and which would also make respectful spiritual support available to those who have a specific preference for solitary practice. As we work towards a future which recognizes such standards, we can open ourselves to the world of knowledge and experience accumulated over time by spiritual leaders of many religions, and by helping professionals.

I strongly recommend that small groups should do the work of raising funds to send key people to training which the group has identified as valuable to them. The training need not be restricted to one leader, e.g., the high priestess of a coven. Some subjects deserve attention by the whole group, perhaps all taking the same workshop or class together. This allows everyone to debrief with each other, discussing how to adapt what is learned to your particular situation. And some subjects are best taught by someone outside the group. An experienced, reputable teacher or trainer will be able to say things that you are uncomfortable addressing with your own group members (or that your group members hesitate to say in front of you!). They will have expertise in facilitating difficult conversations, helping the group come to consensus or at least a decision on important matters. And they can give valuable unbiased post-training feedback about problems they noticed which need special attention, or things which deserve praise. Here are some training recommendations paired with issues the training might address.

Training: Leadership Skills

Can help with group unrest and dissatisfaction, conflicts among group members, stronger programs, better organized events, development of other leaders.

Training: Group Dynamics

Can help with recognizing patterns in your group or group activities, knowing how to stem dysfunction before it takes root or causes harm to your group, prevent dissolution of your group from people leaving to avoid dysfunction. Since group members often have unrealistic expectations of those they look to for leadership, I recommend both leaders and groups should actively pursue training.

Training: Appreciating and Integrating Cultural and Other Types of Diversity

Can help with helping all to feel safe, wanted, welcomed, and included in your activities, including those with different physical or mental abilities. Can enrich the experience of all through learning about others not like themselves. Can protect you from charges of sexual abuse or harassment, and charges of racial, ethnic, gender and other types of discrimination.

Training: About Alcohol and Other Addictions

Can help with your understanding of individuals living with addictions either in themselves or in their families, of those in recovery from addiction and their particular needs, how to make your activities welcoming of people facing these challenges, and how to help people with a problem get the help they need.

Training: About Domestic Violence

Can help with your understanding of people who live with a violent partner or parent, and those who are survivors of abuse, how to support someone living with or fleeing domestic violence, and how to protect your group or activities from becoming victims of a violent person connected to a group member.

Training: About Trauma Issues

Can help with your understanding of how trauma can create PTSD (post-traumatic stress disorder), how to support someone with PTSD, how to get them the professional help they may need.

Training: About Mental Illness

Can help with recognizing potential mental illness in an individual, knowing how to refer them to a mental health professional, understanding how to support and work with someone with mental illness.

Training: Ethics, Personal Boundaries

Can help with establishing your own code of behavior and reasons for your vocation, helping you maintain respectful and appropriate boundaries with others, protecting you and your group from unnecessary controversy or even lawsuit.

Training: Active-Supportive Listening and Other Traditional Chaplaincy Skills

Can help with deepening a richer and more effective ministry to others.

Training: Self-Care and Avoiding Burnout

Can help with your ability to consistently provide services and offer compassionate support without becoming depleted.

During your discernment process, take note of where training could help strengthen an area of vulnerability for you, then identify a way to access good training. If you feel you have no vulnerabilities, then consider a subject about which you are curious and simply want to learn more.

Your Little Black Book

That late night call from a depressed adolescent who seems to be contemplating suicide. The Pagan who used to come to your meetings who suddenly turns up at your door asking about legal resources. The woman in your group who always seems tense and reluctant to speak up around her partner. The middle-aged bachelor who usually smells of alcohol and makes inappropriate jokes about mead, the Great Rite, and what the young women are wearing. Many of these situations will strain one leader's expertise, but in at least some cases, a quick response is crucial.

Education and training will teach you when to dial 911 about an immediate life-or-death scenario. For other matters, you need to have a good list of resources and contacts. Research from your environmental scan should have identified at least some of these resources. Create your own system for pulling out that information in a hurry. My own very simple method is to have a "contact" in my phone and computers called "Referrals." In the notes section I just paste in names and contact information. That way I don't have to remember who it is I need to look up. As mentioned before, Cherry Hill Seminary has a good page of national emergency resources and hotlines that you may want to bookmark (at cherryhillseminary.org under Resources).

Collaborative Constellations

And speaking of resources, having partners and allies is a powerful way of being more effective, amplifying your gravitational field, so to speak. Partners add credibility, support and advise each other, and mitigate the burnout experienced by so many solo ministers and leaders. Partners reinforce with each other's core values, serving as a reminder to always align activities with mission.

Your leadership constellation can be the small group of other Pagans who you trust to take over when you are sick, travelling or just need a break. Even one or two partners can multiply the value of your ministry constellation, possibly attracting new participants through the leaders' array of contacts. Good partners can enhance your reputation; the two or three of you demonstrate to the outside that you value relationships, that you are willing to model how community works.

The points of light in an allies constellation will represent your connections to others in your community who will support you when needed. Some allies are other Pagans; others are contacts you made with referral resources. The people in my interfaith group are strong allies for me and they connect me to much wider circles of influence, partnerships, programs and emotional support. You know who you can trust — be sure you have shared with those special people your ministry plans. Give them a chance to offer help or just to affirm your direction. Think of them as being like an advisory council; there if you need them, non-intrusive when you do not.

One more aspect of this analogy would be the liaisons that occur between constellations. By that, I mean that your group, or group of activities, need not exist in isolation from other groups. If you and your activities are primarily Druid, consider inviting individuals and leaders from other traditions to come together periodically. Preserving a local wetlands, opposing an ordinance against fortune-telling, marching with townspeople against racism on Martin Luther King Day — these are issues around which many Pagans can come together. Getting to know and trust each other while working on shared concerns will make it much easier to bridge differences when something more insidious threatens the commonweal, like the circulation among groups by a suspected sexual predator.

Preparing for Change

How do you know when what you are doing is working? When you should be patient and wait for results? When you should acknowledge the need to release your hold on an aspect of your ministry?

Some of the hard questions that you worked with during your discernment process will have challenged you to determine a strategy for ending an activity or ministry. Each of your activity plans should include a list of benchmarks, the time by which they should occur, and the outcomes required in order to claim success. Regular checks on progress towards these benchmarks is a good exercise to do with partners if you have them, or even with your group.

Take your time, but don't ignore the signs that it's time for a change. An old Scotsman once told me, "Holli, if you are sitting on a cake of ice and it's melting, stay on it. If your backside is freezing, get off!" If there is one constant in twenty-first century life, surely it is change. That requires us to be nimble, developing habits of ongoing adaptation. It includes mentoring and listening to the ideas of younger generations, who will have their own ways. It also means you must prepare someone else to be your replacement should a time come that you cannot or no longer wish to continue what you are doing. Like death, this may come slowly or suddenly, so it's far preferable to plan for it in advance, easing the adjustment for all concerned.

The Shape of Compassion

During the 2020 pandemic the novel coronavirus taught us lessons about community that may have only been abstract before. At this point, we have lived the truth that what happens far away touches each of us in ways we may not anticipate. Now that everything has changed for us, regardless of our social class, race, gender, education, or anything else that commonly denote privilege, effective ministry is more important than ever.

We have also seen the shape of religious communities shaken to the core. Covens, Druid groves, synagogues, and churches—all have been forced to come to terms with what it means to be a community of separate individuals. There has been widespread grieving over the loss of corporate devotional space by many who assumed they would not like Zoom ceremonies. Pagans have usually been early adopters of technology, employing chat, email, and online bulletin boards for ritual use for several decades. In the face of pandemic quarantines and stay-at-home conditions they turned to electronic formats in refreshed forms, utilizing technologies to bring richness to gatherings large and small.

Loneliness, uncertainty, anguish, and grief surprised most of us with an unaccustomed imbalance. In such a time we question our theology, the meaning of our own life, our relationships, indeed, every pattern or form which has until now given shape to our existence. A Pagan minister can be a valuable spiritual companion through unexpected transition.

During the worst of the initial wave of virus-related deaths in New York City in 2020, I attended a nationwide chaplains' web panel. My takeaway (well, one) was this advice to a young chaplain from someone who was then serving in that disastrous setting: "Don't just do something, stand there!" Stand, that is, for what anchors you at your core. Stand quietly, offering your witness to the sacred suffering of others. Stand for peace and balance in a world suddenly topsy-turvy.

We can't fix the world, but we can step up to caring. The pandemic rendered (at least for a time) many of our differences moot and irrelevant. When such obstacles disintegrate, we are better able to focus on what we do have in common—our shared life as part of Gaia, our shared love for each other, our concern for those in pain or fear.

Chapter 6

Vision for the Future

What will be required of Pagan ministers in the future? I have asked myself this question many times, particularly while writing *Constellated Ministry*, but I am no prophet, no seer. I do know this: the things that remain unchanged are the human spirit, the search for meaning, the need for compassion, and the desire to serve. I believe that these deserve more flexible, responsive frameworks for support.

If there are growing numbers who have been disenchanted and disappointed by their former religions, then I say those who had negative, boring, rigid, judgmental experiences were victims of mediocrity, a cautionary tale to Pagans not to recreate mediocrity in simply a different flavor. Imagining a new paradigm does not come easily, nor expeditiously. Nevertheless, we need a vision for the future with constellations of smoothly functioning Pagan networks which nurture and support the spirituality of new generations of Pagans.

Third-century Buddhists imagined the cosmos in the form of a great net cast across the sky. Jewels of perfect and infinite clarity formed each intersection of this net of living connections. Every point reflected all the other celestial jewels, so that each one contained and revealed the perfection of all the jewels. They called this interconnected web Indra's Net. Comparing this image to that of contemporary Paganism, I am struck, not just by the connections, but also by the fact that each jewel reflects all of the others. So often, we Pagans have been islands when we had hoped to be oases. But here is a model of quality, flexibility, clarity and mutual support—a ministry constellation.

Over the years, I have encountered much cynicism among Pagans, and it is not specific to locale or demography, but occurs everywhere that people are disappointed and hurt. The voices of the Pagan leaders featured in Chapter 4 give me hope for a stronger, happier future for our overall religious world. We often assert that Paganism is the antidote to the world's toxicity, a path for understanding our relationship with the planetary and human ecosystems. If we believe these things are true, we have a sacred duty to press forward, building the spiritual future that we wish to inhabit. This involves the recommendations made in the last chapter, particularly training and the building of supportive networks.

The introduction noted Pagans' problematic relationship with terms like ministry. My hope is that readers will resist the impulse to be put off by language they perceive as reminiscent of past disillusionment. Pagans have reclaimed words like witch and heathen, which were emblems of disrepute for centuries. I hope the same strategy of constructing fresh meanings can help ministers—the ones who cannot look away from need—re-envision what ministry can look like.

By shifting the focus of ministry away from a location, and away from one individual, the concept of constellated ministry has described a way we can live into an uncertain future. Every location, every leader, are still bright lights in their constellation, but with a different paradigm for ministry, it is easier for us to see

Vision for the Future

them crossing lines that may in the past have represented boundaries. These boundaries of territory and personality are no longer needed, if individuals will see themselves as part of a dynamic whole. The observed edges of a constellation may be useful for the leader assessing their own capacity. But for others the stars can regroup into new constellations which enfold them even when their lives, and needs, change over time.

Just a few nights ago I dreamed I stood at an arrival point for buses full of people seeking help, much like some Red Cross disaster operations I've attended. The people were quiet, waiting patiently for direction, but their faces were anxious, lined with insecurity. I could almost read a caption bubble over their heads saying that they feared change. In my dream I was explaining to my supervisor that even if these individuals were not injured or put out of their homes by a hurricane or fire, they were nonetheless needing our support just because of the stress in their lives. When I woke, I felt sorrow to recognize that every one of us is in one of those buses. And each of us deserves a spiritual companion while facing the uncertainty of modern life.

I close with the reminder that most people, including Pagans, still consider themselves religious, spiritual, or feeling that there is a meaning beyond physical existence. At some point in their lives, most Pagans are likely to feel the need for spiritual support, even while they are still defining themselves and their religion. The unique nature of Pagan culture calls for new ways of ministry adapted to Pagan needs and concerns. It is my hope that this book will stimulate ideas, provoke conversation, and help to build resiliency and effectiveness for Pagan groups as well as solitaries, in the process, strengthening the overall fabric of our communal spiritual life.

Resources

Addictions
Collins, Cynthia Jane. *The Recovery Spiral: A Pagan Path to Healing*. New York: Citadel, 2004.
Hebert, Deirdre A. *The Pagan in Recovery: The Twelve Steps from a Pagan Perspective*. Hubbardston, Mass.: Asphodel Press, 2011.

Conflict in Religious Groups
Haugk, Kenneth C. *Antagonists in the Church: How to Identify and Deal with Destructive Conflict*. Minneapolis: Augsburg Publishing House, 1988.

Group Needs
Free Management Library
https://managementhelp.org/

Pagan Consent Culture
http://www.paganconsentculture.com/p/consent-culture.html

Cultural Appropriation
Handout by Anti-Oppression Resource & Training Alliance (AORTA)
https://aorta.coop/portfolio_page/cultural-appropriation/
Empowering Young People in the Aftermath of Hate (In English and en Español)

What Educators and Family Members Can Do
https://www.adl.org/education/resources/tools-and-strategies/empowering-young-people-in-the-aftermath-of-hate-in

Mental Health
Mental Health information by topic
https://medlineplus.gov/mentalhealthandbehavior.html

Resources 121

National Suicide Prevention Lifeline
https://suicidepreventionlifeline.org/

Military Needs

Tick, Edward. *War and the Soul.* Wheaton, Illinois: Quest Books, 2005.
PTSD: National Center for PTSD
https://www.ptsd.va.gov/

Prison Ministry

O'Gaia, Ashleen, and Garr, Carol. *Enchantment Encumbered: The Study and Practice of Wicca in Restricted Environments.* CreateSpace Independent Publishing, 2009.

Prisoner Community Re-Entry

https://www.justice.gov/archive/fbci/progmenu_reentry.html
Managing Sex Offenders in the Community
https://nationalreentryresourcecenter.org/circles-of-support-and-accountability/

Victim Support Services

https://victimsupportservices.org/help-for-victims/what-is-a-victim-advocate/

Violence at Home

Don't Look Away: Recognizing & Responding to Abuse for non-professionals.
Free media presentation available for download
https://cherryhillseminary.org/wp-content/uploads/2014/04/Dont-Look-Away.ppsx

Understanding and Preventing Child Abuse and Neglect

https://www.apa.org/pi/families/resources/understanding-child-abuse

National Center for Missing & Exploited Children

https://www.missingkids.org/home

National Child Traumatic Stress Network

https://www.nctsn.org/resources

National Resource Center on Domestic Violence

https://www.nrcdv.org/

Violence in the Community

Gun Violence and Mass Shootings (for Parents, Families and Caregivers)
https://www.adl.org/education/resources/tools-and-strategies/table-talk/gun-violence-mass-shootings

Bibliography

Beaumont, Susan. *How to Lead When You Don't Know Where You're Going: Leading in a Liminal Season.* Lanham, Md.: Rowman & Littlefield, 2019.

Bellah, Robert N., Richard Madsen, William M. Sullivan, Ann Swidler, and Steven M. Tipton. *Habits of the Heart: Individualism and Commitment in American Life.* Berkeley: University of California Press, 2007.

Berger, Helen A., "Are Solitaries The Future Of Paganism?" Patheos.com, August, 23, 2010, https://www.patheos.com/resources/additional-resources/2010/08/solitaries-the-future-of-paganism.

Berger, Helen A. *A Community of Witches: Contemporary Neo-paganism and Witchcraft in the United States.* Columbia: University of South Carolina Press, 1999.

Berger, Helen A., Evan A. Leach, and Leigh S. Shaffer *Voices from the Pagan Census: A National Survey of Witches and Neo-pagans in the United States.* Columbia: University of South Carolina Press, 2013.

Berkeley, George. "Moral Attraction." In *The Works of George Berkeley Volume 3*, edited by Alexander Campbell Fraser, 189. London: Macmillan and Co., 1861.

Bidwell, Duane R. *When One Religion Isn't Enough: The Lives of Spiritually Fluid People.* Boston: Beacon Press, 2018.

Brenner, Joanna, and Aaron Smith. *72 percent of Online Adults are Social Networking Site Users.* Pew Research Center, 2013.

Cadge, Wendy, and Michelle A. Scheidt. *Meditations on Chaplaincy and Spiritual Care: A Conversation with Chaplains Across Settings.* Chaplaincy Innovation Lab and Fetzer Institute, 2020. http://chaplaincyinnovation.org/resources/meditations.

Campbell, H. A., and Alessandra Vitullo. "Assessing Changes in the Study of Religious Communities in Digital Religion Studies," *Church, Communication and Culture* 1, no. 1 (2016), 73–89. https://doi.org/10.1080/23753234.2016.1181301.

Campbell, Heidi. "Internet and Religion: The Handbook of Internet Studies." In *Internet and Religion: The Handbook of Internet Studies,* edited by Mia Consalvo and Charles Ess, 232–50. Wiley Online Library, 2011.

Chayko, Mary. "The Portable Community: Envisioning and Examining Mobile Social Connectedness," *International Journal of Web Based Communities* 3, no. 4 (2007), 373–85. https://doi.org/10.1504/ijwbc.2007.015864.

Clifton, Chas S. *Her Hidden Children: The Rise of Wicca and Paganism in America.* Lanham, Md.: AltaMira, 2006.

Coco, Angela. "Pagan Religiousness as 'Networked Individualism,'" In *Spirituality: Theory, Praxis and Pedagogy*, edited by Robert Fisher and Daniel Riha, 125–36. Leiden: Brill, 2012.

Coco, Angela. "Pagans Online and Offline: Locating Community in Postmodern Times." *Sociological Spectrum* 28, no. 5 (2008), 510–30. https://doi.org/10.1080/02732170802206138.

Cowan, Douglas E., *Cyberhenge: Modern Pagans on the Internet.* London: Routledge, 2004.

Cunningham, Scott. *Magical Herbalism: The Secret Craft of the Wise.* Woodbury, Minn.: Llewellyn Publications, 1982.

Durkheim, Emile. *The Elementary Forms of the Religious Life, A Study in Religious Sociology.* London: G. Allen & Unwin, 1915.

Emore, Holli. *Group or Solitary: Choice and Spiritual Care Needs in Contemporary Paganism.* Columbia, S.C.: Cherry Hill Seminary, 2018.

Ezzy, Douglas. "The Commodification of Witchcraft." *Australian Religion Studies Review* 14, no. 1 (2001), 31–44.

Ezzy, Douglas, and Helen A. Berger. "Witchcraft: Changing Patterns of Participation in the Early Twenty-First Century," *The Pomegranate: The International Journal of Pagan Studies* 11, no. 2 (2009), 165–80. https://doi.org/10.1558/pome.v11i2.165.

Funk, Cary, and April Clark. *Americans and Social Trust: Who, Where and Why.* Washington, D.C.: Pew Social Trends, 2007.

Funk, Cary, and Greg Smith. "'Nones' on the Rise." Washington, D.C.: Pew Forum on Religion & Public Life, 2012.

Giordan, Giuseppe, and Enzo Pace. *Mapping Religion and Spirituality in a Postsecular World.* Leiden: Brill, 2012. https://doi.org/10.1163/9789004230231.

Harvey, Graham. *Contemporary Paganism: Listening People, Speaking Earth.* New York: NYU Press, 2000.

Haugk, Kenneth C. *Antagonists in the Church: How to Identify and Deal with Destructive Conflict.* Minneapolis: Augsburg, 1988.

Heim, S. M. "Of Two Minds about a Theology without Walls." *Journal of Ecumenical Studies* 51, no. 4 (2017), 479–86. https://doi.org/10.1353/ecu.2016.0043.

Hill, Robert L. *The Complete Guide to Small Group Ministry: Saving the World Ten at a Time.* Boston: Skinner House, 2003.

Hutton, Ronald. *The Triumph of the Moon: A History of Modern Pagan Witchcraft.* Oxford: Oxford University Press, 1999.

Kosmin, B. A., and Ariela Keysar. *American Nones: The Profile of the No Religion Population.* Hartford, Conn.: Institute for the Study of Secularism in Society & Culture, 2009.

Lave, Jean, and Etienne Wenger. *Situated Learning: Legitimate Peripheral Participation.* Cambridge: Cambridge University Press, 1991. https://doi.org/10.1017/cbo9780511815355.

Lewis, James R. "Cracks in the Network Conversion Paradigm." *International Journal for the Study of New Religions* 3, no. 2 (2012), 143–62.

Lewis, James R. "The Pagan Explosion Revisited: A Statistical Postmortem on the Teen Witch Fad," *The Pomegranate: The International Journal of Pagan Studies* 14, no. 2 (2012), 128–39. https://doi.org/10.1558/pome.v14i1.128.

Lewis, James R., and Inga Tollefsen. "Gender and Paganism in Census and Survey Data." *The Pomegranate: The International Journal of Pagan Studies* 15 (2013), 61–78. https://doi.org/10.1558/pome.v15i1-2.61.

Linzie, Bill. *Reconstructionism's Role in Modern Heathenry*, 2007. Licensed under the Creative Commons (USA) Attribution-NoDerivs 3.0 Unported. http://www.angelfire.com/nm/seidhman/reconstruction-c.pdf.

Luhrmann, Tanya M. "Why Going to Church Is Good for You." *The New York Times*, April 20, 2013.

Magliocco, Sabina. *Witching Culture: Folklore and Neo-Paganism in America.* Philadelphia: University of Pennsylvania Press, 2010.

Marler, Penny L., and C. Kirk Hadaway. "Being Religious or Being Spiritual in America: A Zero-Sum Proposition?" *Journal for the Scientific Study of Religion* 41, no. 2 (2002), 289–300. https://doi.org/10.1111/1468-5906.00117.

McClure, Paul. "Tinkering with Technology and Religion in the Digital Age: The Effects of Internet Use on Religious Belief, Behavior, and Belonging," *Journal for the Scientific Study of Religion,* 56, no. 3 (2017), 481–97. https://doi.org/10.1111/jssr.12365.

McGee, LaDorna. *Participation, Identity, and Social Support in A Spiritual Community.* MA thesis, University of Texas Arlington, December 2005.

Mercadante, Linda. *Belief without Borders: Inside the Minds of the Spiritual but not Religious.* Oxford: Oxford University Press, 2014.

Mercadante, Linda. "How Does it Fit? Multiple Religious Belonging, Spiritual but not Religious, and the Dances of Universal Peace," *Open Theology* 3, no. 1 (2017), 10–18. https://doi.org/10.1515/opth-2017-0002.

Mercadante, Linda. "The Seeker Next Door: What Drives the 'Spiritual but Not Religious,'" *Christianity Today*, May 18, 2012. www.faithformationlearningexchange.net.

Merriam, Sharan, Bradley Courtenay, and Lisa Baumgartner. "On Becoming a Witch: Learning in a Marginalized Community of Practice." *Adult Education Quarterly* 53, no. 3 (2003), 170–88. https://doi.org/10.1177/0741713603053003003.

Minister, Kevin. "Transforming Introductory Courses in Religion: From World Religions to Interreligious Studies." In *Interreligious/Interfaith Studies: Defining a New Field*, edited by Eboo Patel, Jennifer Howe Peace, and Noah J. Silverman, 60–71. Boston: Beacon Press, 2018.

Patel, Eboo, Jennifer Howe Peace, and Noah J. Silverman, eds. *Interreligious/Interfaith Studies: Defining a New Field*. Boston: Beacon Press, 2018.

Pike, Sarah. *Earthly Bodies, Magical Selves: Contemporary Pagans and the Search for Community*. Berkeley: University of California Press, 2001. https://www.degruyter.com/california/view/title/555120.

Putnam, Robert D., and David E Campbell. *American Grace: How Religion Divides and Unites Us*. New York: Simon and Schuster, 2010.

Ravenswood, Scarlet. "Why There Are So Many Solitary Female Pagans: The Hard Truth." *Arcane Alchemy* blog. June 21, 2017. www.arcane-alchemy.com.

Reece, Gwendolyn. "Impediments to Practice in Contemporary Paganism," *The Pomegranate: The International Journal of Pagan Studies* 16, no. 2 (2014): 150–77. https://doi.org/10.1558/pome.v16i2.27020.

Reece, Gwendolyn. "Prevalence and Importance of Contemporary Pagan Practices," *The Pomegranate: The International Journal of Pagan Studies* 16, no. 1 (2014): 35–54. https://doi.org/10.1558/pome.v16i1.20231.

Reece, Gwendolyn. "Contemporary Pagans and Stigmatized Identity," *The Pomegranate: The International Journal of Pagan Studies* 18, no. 1 (2016): 60–95. https://doi.org/10.1558/pome.v18i1.27917.

Reid, Sian. "WITCH WARS: Factors Contributing to Conflict in Canadian Neopagan Communities," *The Pomegranate: The International Journal of Pagan Studies* 11 (2000): 10–20. https://doi.org/10.1558/pome.v13i10.10.

Roof, Wade Clark. *Spiritual Marketplace: Baby Boomers and the Remaking of American Religion*. Princeton: Princeton University Press, 2001.
Smith, S.G., X. Zhang, K.C. Basile, M.T. Merrick, J. Wang, M. Kresnow, J. Chen. *The National Intimate Partner and Sexual Violence Survey (NISVS): 2015 Data Brief – Updated Release*. Atlanta: National Center for Injury Prevention and Control, Centers for Disease Control and Prevention, 2018.
Smith, Tom W., Peter Marsden, Michael Hout, and Jibum Kim. "Religion & Spirituality: Religious Preference," *General Social Survey*, 2016. https://gssdataexplorer.norc.org.
Snook, Jennifer. *American Heathens: The Politics of Identity in a Pagan Religious Movement*. Philadelphia: Temple University Press, 2015. https://doi.org/10.2307/j.ctvrdf42h.
Streib, Heinz, and Ralph W. Wood. "'Spirituality' as Privatized Experience-Oriented Religion: Empirical and Conceptual Perspectives," *Implicit Religion* 14, no. 4 (2011), 433–53. https://doi.org/10.1558/imre.v14i4.433.
Strmiska, Michael. *Modern Paganism in World Cultures: Comparative Perspectives*. Santa Barbara, Calif.: ABC-Clio, 2005.
Ter Kuile, Casper, and Angie Thurston. "Where We Belong: Mapping American Religious Innovation." 2015. http://fetzer.org.
Tick, Edward. *War and the Soul: Healing Our Nation's Veterans from Post-traumatic Stress Disorder*. Wheaton, Illinois: Quest Books, 2005.
Tocqueville, Alexis de. *Democracy in America*. Washington, D.C.: Regnery Publishing, 2003.
Truman, Jennifer, and Rachel Morgan. *Nonfatal Domestic Violence, 2003–2012*. U.S. Department of Justice Office of Justice Programs, April 2014.
Twenge, Jean M., Ryne A. Sherman, Julie J. Exline, and Joshua B. Grubbs. "Declines in American Adults' Religious Participation and Beliefs, 1972–2014." *Sage Open* 6, no. 1 (2016). https://doi.org/10.1177/2158244016638133.
U.S. Census Bureau. *Annual Estimates of the Resident Population: April 1, 2010 to July 1, 2016*," (n.d.). https://factfinder.census.gov.
Van Gulik, Léon A. "Cleanliness is Next to Godliness, But Oaths are for Horses: Antecedents and Consequences of the Institutionalization of Secrecy in Initiatory Wicca," *The Pomegranate: The International Journal of Pagan Studies* 14, no. 2 (2012), 233–55.
Waldron, David. "Witchcraft for Sale! Commodity vs. Community in the Neopagan Movement," *Nova Religio* 9, no. 1 (2005): 32–48. https://doi.org/10.1525/nr.2005.9.1.032.

Wellman, Barry. "The Persistence and Transformation of Community: From Neighbourhood Groups to Social Networks." October 31, 2001.

Wenger, Etienne. "Communities of Practice: A Brief Introduction." In *STEP Leadership Workshop*, University of Oregon, 2011. http://scholarsbank.uoregon.edu.

Wenger, Etienne. "Communities of Practice: The Organizational Frontier," February 2000, www.rareplanet.org.

Wuthnow, Robert. *I Come Away Stronger: How Small Groups are Shaping American Religion.* Grand Rapids: Eerdmans, 1994.

Wuthnow, Robert. *Loose Connections: Joining Together in America's Fragmented Communities.* Cambridge, Mass.: Harvard University Press, 2002.

Wuthnow, Robert. "Small Groups Forge New Notions of Community and the Sacred," *The Christian Century*, February 1994. www.religion-online.org.

Ysseldyk, Renate, Kimberly Matheson, and Hymie Anisman. "Religiosity as Identity: Toward an Understanding of Religion From a Social Identity Perspective," *Personality and Social Psychology Review* 14, no. 1 (2010), 60–71.

Appendix : Group or Solitary: Choices and Spiritual Care Needs in Contemporary Pagan Practice

As both a minister and a seminary educator I have for years been curious about why the majority of Pagans surveyed in western countries say they are solitary. The fact of the predominance of solitary practice had been well-established by both Helen Berger and, later, Gwendolyn Reece. I wanted to find out why, and whether it was a choice, or simply the only option available for most. The Pagan Engagement and Spiritual Support Survey undertook to discover some answers to these questions, as well as just what it is that Pagans want, or perceive that they need, from spiritual support resources like a group, a priest/ess, or other kind of minister. Since the report of that study is not widely available to the public, it is adapted and abridged here as an appendix for readers who wish to see the specific results.

Pagan Engagement and Spiritual Support Survey

The research problem noted that education and training for Pagan ministry are currently uninformed by any kind of best practices specific to the unique culture of Paganism. Such best practices must be supported by research. The Pagan Engagement and Spiritual Support Survey sought to collect data about why some Pagans affiliate with a local group and others identify themselves as solitary, what are their spiritual support needs, and how do they prefer to access spiritual support.

Survey Responses

Question 2 asked for personal religious or spiritual identification which might allow comparison to other national surveys, such as the Pew Forum on Religion & Public Life. The largest category chosen was "Spiritual" (51.9 percent), followed by 21.7 percent who selected "SBNR," or a total of 73.6 percent combined "Spiritual" or "SBNR." Only 16.2 percent considered themselves "Religious," 5.3 percent "None of the above," and 4.8 percent "Humanist." "Witch" or "Wiccan" was the predominant self-identification in the most recent previous survey,[44] at more than 90 percent, though these numbers are difficult to evaluate since respondents were allowed to name more than one religious tradition.

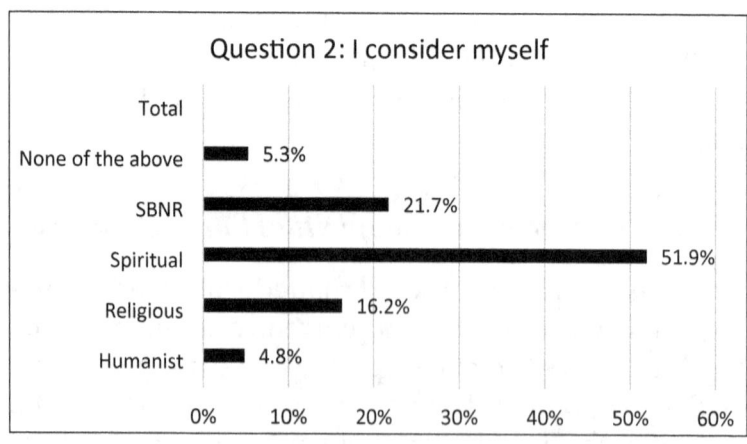

---

44 Reece, Gwendolyn. "Prevalence and Importance of Contemporary Pagan Practices," *The Pomegranate: The International Journal of Pagan Studies* 16, no. 1 (2014): 41.

A significant number (45.5 percent) indicated "I do not practice with a regular group," while 28.3 percent chose "I currently practice with or attend a regular group." "I used to practice with or attend a regular group but not at present" was chosen by 21.9 percent. Only 4.3 percent selected the response, "I am part of a group which meets regularly online." (Figure 2)

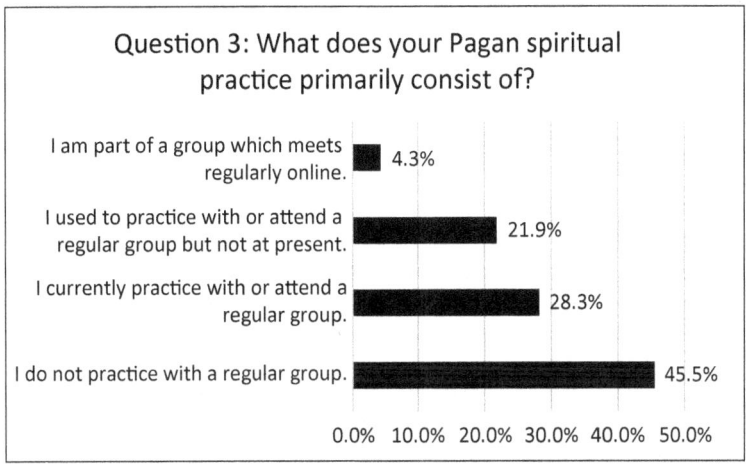

Asked for one or more reasons a respondent may be part of a group, the largest group (61.4 percent) responded, "Opportunity to learn and grow from and with others in the group," closely followed by "Social bonds with other members" (54.4 percent). "I do not practice with a group" was selected by 31.9 percent, and 24.5 percent chose "[It's] more effective to practice as a group."

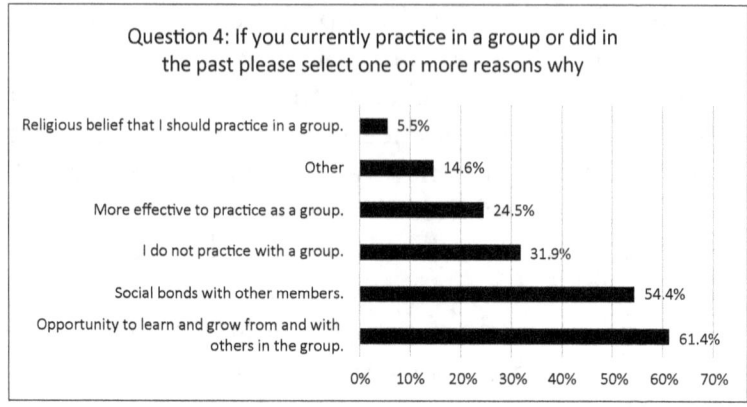

Question 5 allowed all respondents to select three reasons they think some Pagans are solitary. The largest group of responses were the 64.7 percent who selected, "They can't find a group near them," and the 62.2 percent who chose, "They would rather be solitary." The next cluster of responses were: "They haven't found meaningful practice in a group" (40 percent); "They can't find a group in their tradition" (34.9 percent); "They have had disagreements with groups or their leaders" (31.6 percent); and "Easier to fit [being solitary] in a busy work schedule" (30.7 percent).

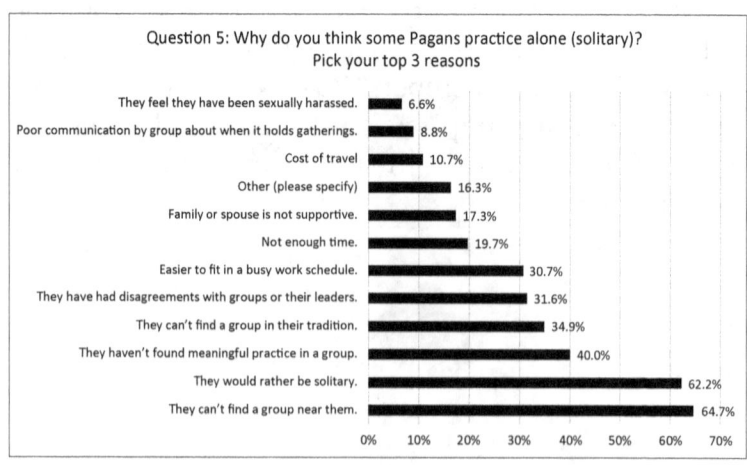

Respondents were asked what the best way to find a group was. "Online listings" was selected by 21 percent as the best way to find a Pagan group, and "Social media" by 17.4 percent. "I don't know" was the choice of 18.6 percent, and "Word of mouth" by 15.7 percent. Some "Other" participants indicated "A Unitarian Universalist Church (CUUPS) group" (7.9 percent), "Notice at an occult store" (5.6 percent), or "There's not a good way" (5 percent).

Those who have not practiced in a group were invited to write in a comment explaining the main reason for their solitary status. As in Question 5 to all participants, the largest category selected was "Hard to find a group near me," (22.9 percent), closely followed by "Hard to find a group that fits" (21.1 percent), and "Prefer solitary practice" (18 percent). Social anxiety, discomfort in groups or introversion were reasons given by 10 percent of participants. Personality cults, poor leadership and internal group conflict were reasons given by 8.4 percent.

The majority (74.4 percent) make use of online access to spiritual resources or groups, while 12.6 percent do not. A few (.4 percent) indicated limited internet access, while 7 percent indicated the need for information on where to go online for such connections. "Other" comments were given by 5.6 percent of participants and were textually-analyzed by the researcher. Of these comments, 55.4 percent wrote that they "occasionally" go online for such contacts, 19.6 percent "seldom" do so, and 13 percent mentioned Facebook.

A large number of participants (72.1 percent) would attend a local group in person if possible, 10.7 percent were "Unsure," 7.9 percent were "Unlikely," 3.6 percent would do so "Only if it is in my tradition," and

5.8 percent wrote comments in "Other." The largest categories of "Other" comments included, "Disabled, health issues or lack transportation" (8.4 percent of comments), and "I'd only go occasionally (4.2 percent of comments).

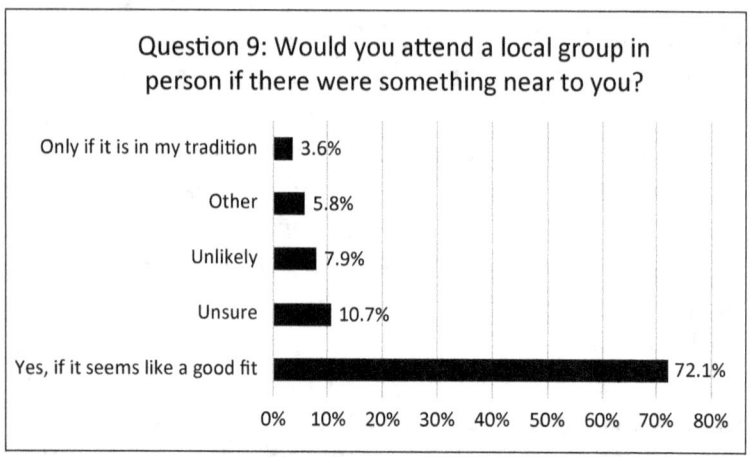

Asked what changes in a former group might attract their return to the group, the largest group (19.7 percent) chose "Other" and wrote in a comment. Comment categories included: disbanded former group (15.4 percent); refusal to go back (7.7 percent); group dynamics and purpose (6.5 percent); better leadership (6.5 percent); concerns about bullying, unwanted sex, drugs or fighting (5.8 percent); or improved spiritual experience (4 percent).

Question 11 invited those who prefer to be solitary to explain why they do so (Figure 6). Of the 901 who gave a reason: 14.9 percent prefer autonomy; 14.4 percent wrote that groups are inconvenient, taking too much time and energy; 14.4 percent indicated groups as a poor fit with personal beliefs; 14.1 percent indicated avoidance of group dysfunction and abuse; 13.2

percent prefer being alone; 10.3 percent say they have a better connection to the sacred when solitary; 7 percent mention social anxiety; and 6.1 percent have a desire for privacy.

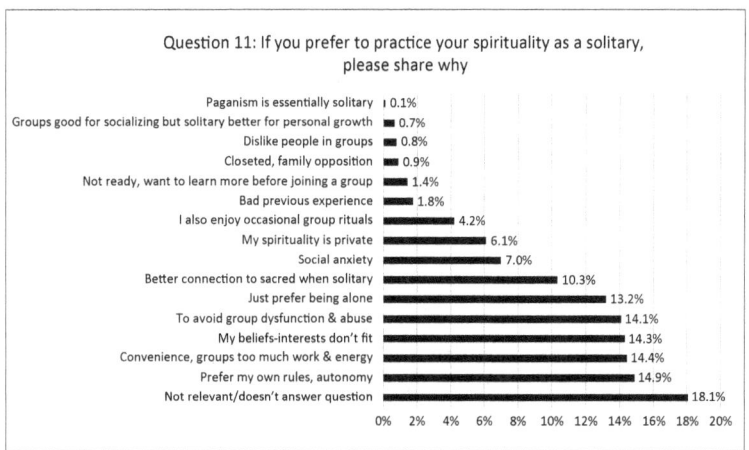

Questions 12 through 15 ask for information about spiritual support resources of the respondents, and their experiences with spiritual support in the past. Most participants (73.8 percent) chose, "Exploring and going deeper with my spirituality," as a reason they might seek spiritual support. "Wedding, handfasting, funeral/memorial services, etc." were selected by 48.2 percent, "Life stresses like employment, family or health issues" by 46.1 percent, "Learning about my tradition," by 37.4 percent, and "None" by 6.4 percent. Comment themes included: learning and discussion (14.5 percent of comments); deeper connection to community (13.2 percent of comments); emotional support and friendship (12.6 percent of comments); and to hold group rituals, initiations, ordinations (7.5 percent of comments).

Question 13 asked participants to whom they would primarily turn for spiritual support (Figure 7). The most common response (36 percent) was "Friend or family member," followed by: "Another member of my group" (15 percent); "I don't know" (10.5 percent); "Someone online" (10.2 percent); "My group leader" (9.8 percent); "A leader or teacher in another group" (5.2 percent); and "A mental health professional (3.6 percent). Of the 9.4 percent who selected "Other" these themes were indicated among the comments: "no one" 23.8 percent; nature or deity(ies) 23 percent; inner self, prayer, meditation or divination 5.1 percent; a leadership peer 9.5 percent; books and literature 9.5 percent; participant's Unitarian Universalist minister or friends 9.5 percent; a mentor-teacher 7.9 percent; and online resources 7.9 percent.

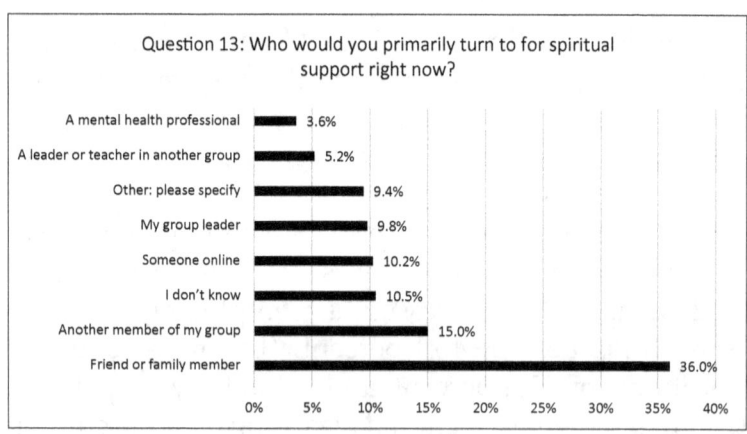

Those who have received spiritual support in the past were invited to explain what the participant had found helpful. The most common categories of comment were "listening, wisdom, experience, empathy" (22.4 percent) and "affirmation, emotional support, not feeling alone" (11.7 percent). Other comments categories were: discussion, social media, music, reading (10.7 percent); non-judgmental approach (9.4 percent); prayer, song, ritual, divination (6.8 percent); and someone who understands my Paganism or worldview (5.9 percent).

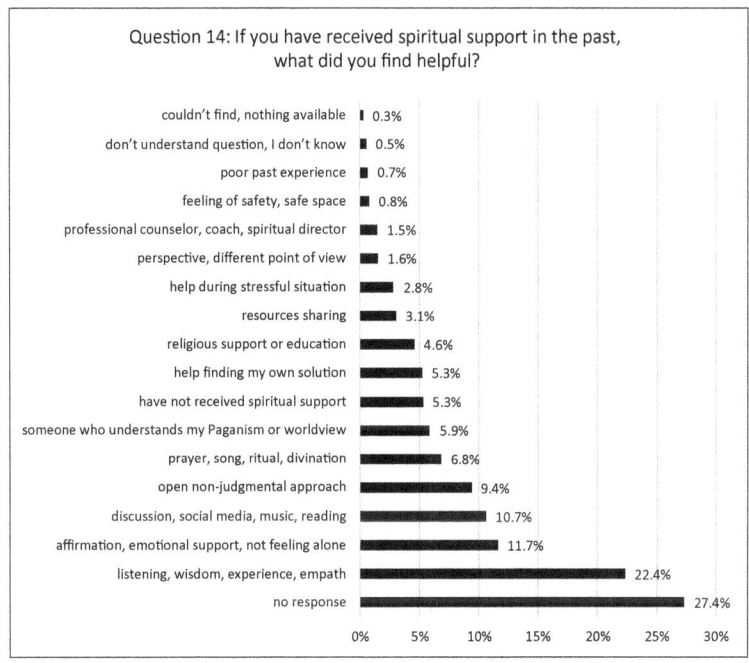

Comments about spiritual support which had not been helpful, (Figure 9), included: poor or ineffective support (18.3 percent); a dogmatic or rigid provider (6.7 percent); a judgmental or blaming provider (6.6 percent); imposition of the provider's personal spirituality or beliefs (5.5 percent); a condescending or dismissive provider (5.2 percent); and an unqualified provider (4 percent).

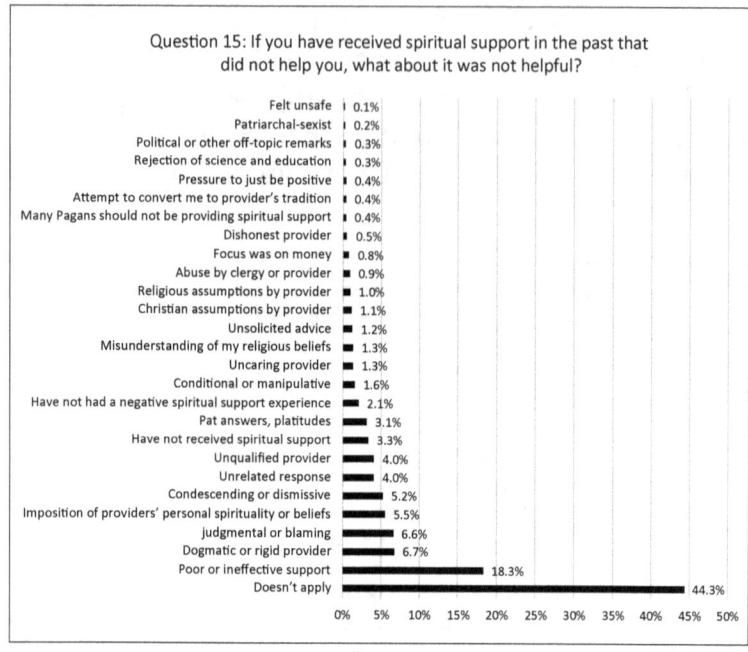

Demographic Information

The remaining survey questions ask for demographic information: specific religious-spiritual identity; state of residence; gender identity; age; and educational attainment.

Participants could write in their religious identification for Question 16. Most responses mentioned multiple religions and influences. Witchcraft or Wicca was mentioned by 46.5 percent, Christian by 35.6 percent; Pagan by 30.9 percent, European-derived by 11.5 percent, and Heathen by 7.1 percent.

Survey respondents identified themselves as 72.8 percent female, 18.5 percent male, 4.3 percent as other, and 4.4 percent no answer. Those of age in their thirties and forties were the largest group, at 23.6 percent and 25.4 percent, respectively, followed by fifties (20.4 percent) and sixties (11.6 percent). Responses were received from a broad sample representing every U.S. state (Figure 17). Indications of the highest level of education achieved (Figure 20) included 5 percent with a doctoral degree, 20.2 percent a graduate degree, 27.9 percent a bachelor degree, 22.2 percent some college but no degree, 4.2 percent a high school degree or equivalent. Some responses were received from individuals who had not yet completed high school (.7 percent), and from others who wrote comments about non-formal training received (4 percent). An informal analysis of all who mentioned Druid, Heathen or Ásatru, or Witch-Wicca, produced the information in the following table.

Religious ID by gender	Other		Male		Female	
Witch	22	3.3 percent	99	14.9 percent	544	81.8 percent
Heathen	13	11.8 percent	35	31.8 percent	62	56.4 percent
Druid	1	1.0 percent	37	35.2 percent	67	63.8 percent

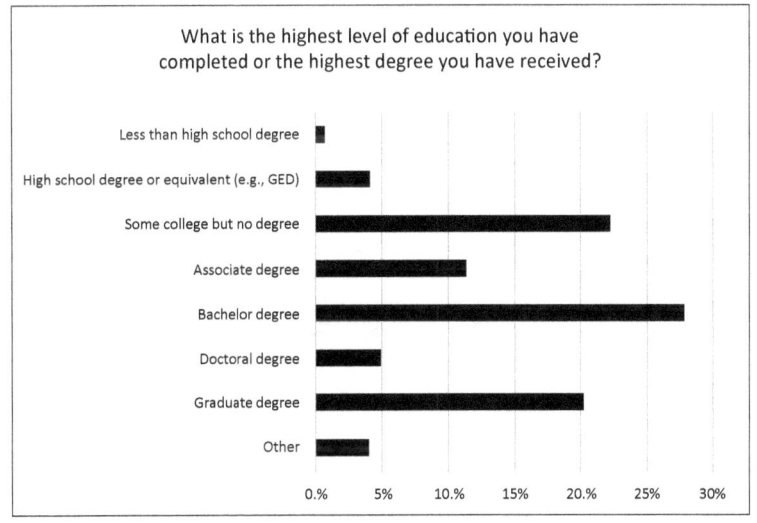

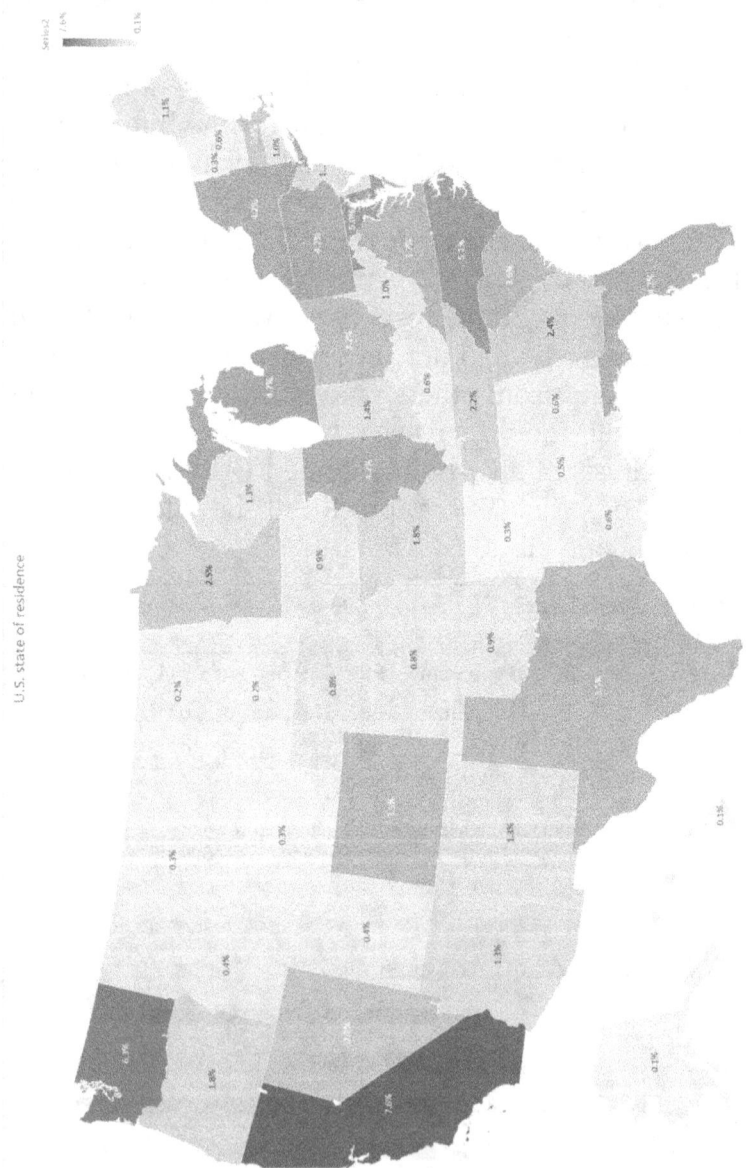

Research Questions Results

This section applies data from survey questions to the research questions. Most questions allowed open comments, generating hundreds of such responses. Selected comment data is given in this research questions section.

Research Question 1: Why do some Pagans choose to be part of a spiritual group and others do not (solitaries)?

Participants indicated that 28.3 percent of them "currently practice with or attend a regular group." (Figure 2) Since the question gave instructions, "Note: this survey uses the word "group" to indicate an in-person gathering local to you," all other responses (71.7 percent) were isolated as "non-group" members. This "non-group" data was then compared to those who indicated their preference for solitary practice in Question 11. There were 90 participants who added comments noting the importance of finding a balance between solitary and group practice.

To answer the research question—why do some Pagans choose to be part of a group and some choose to be solitary?—I categorized comments from several questions, including solitary respondents as well as those who indicated they were part of a group. The most common themes to emerge, in order of prevalence, were: poor group dynamics and leadership; personal preference for autonomy or personal belief; and practical issues such as babysitting, disabilities, time commitment, or cost.

One respondent wrote, "Some people find the immediacy and fluidity of personal practice to be a more honest expression [of] their spirituality." (Survey participant 6537674499) Others pointed out the complementarity of tandem private and group practice, as well as the greater ability to focus, e.g., in meditation, when alone. Several wrote that by being solitary they have learned more sensitivity and awareness of "spirit," or their own "inner voice," which had been damaged by past group participation.

Issues of racism (.7 percent of all responders), fears of emotional abuse and group dysfunction (2.6 percent Question 5, 14.1 percent Question 11), and sexual harassment (6.6 percent in Question 5, 2.9 percent in Question 10) were given as reasons to avoid groups. Ten of the individuals (.6 percent of all responders) who brought up racism said they had left or avoided a group because of its racist leanings, while two (.1 percent of all responders) voiced their belief in racially-segregated Pagan practice. One person used the word "safe" to describe solitary practice. Some concerns involved the fear of being publicly exposed as Pagan (5.9 percent Question 5) if participating in a group.

In addition to those who said health restrictions and disabilities affected their group participation, 7.8 percent (Question 5) of respondents said they were averse to group practice because of introversion, social anxiety, or other related issues. Some individuals mentioned that they are diagnosed as autistic, have past trauma from sexual assault, or diagnosed mental illness.

Research Question 2: What changes, if any, would motivate an unaffiliated Pagan to affiliate with a local group?

At least 58 percent percent of non-group respondents to Question 9, "Would you attend a local group if there were something near you?" (responses by those not currently in a group) indicated that they would consider group involvement, "[I]f it seems like a good fit," plus 2.2 percent who selected the response, "Only if it is in my tradition." Another 18.9 percent of the group were "Unsure," if they would participate in a group, and 12.4 percent were "Unlikely."

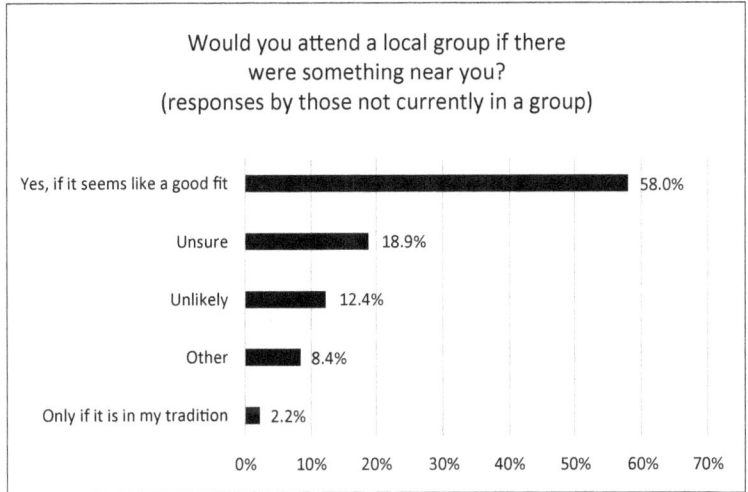

Factors given which might improve the likelihood of group attendance included: transportation (2.4 percent); no sexual harassment (2.9 percent); more convenient meeting time (4.9 percent) or place (5 percent); more diversity (6.1 percent); more transparency (7.1 percent); absence of certain member(s) (7.6 percent); a new leader (9.8 percent); and better organization (13 percent). Twenty-five people noted that they would not return.

Some comments conveyed a natural attenuation away from group participation, as voiced by this respondent:

> I did not leave my former group or my tradition. I simply evolved into a new place in my spiritual life, a place in which the constraints of being in a group and even

running a group based in one tradition felt wrong to me. My mission in the world changed (or, perhaps, evolved) and now I am ripening—preparing to start another tradition that will do its part to help create a new kind of world, and help humanity, as a whole, evolve in at least some small way. (Survey participant 6532822264)

Research Question 3: Does a significant portion of solitary Pagans identify as spiritual but not religious?

Most survey respondents (51.9 percent) chose to describe themselves as "Spiritual" (Figure 1); 21.7 percent selected "Spiritual but Not Religious" (SBNR), and 16.2 percent chose "Religious." Many (316) added comments to clarify their choice, or to explicate their choice of "None of the above." Most (61.1 percent) of those who added comments wrote an explanation of their personal beliefs or tradition; 33.5 percent of commenters wrote that they were "Spiritual and Religious," and 11.1 percent wrote that it was difficult to choose just one label.

Spiritual identity choices were also analyzed by group participation or non-group (Figure 13). Among the individuals practicing with or attending a group, 13.9 percent identified themselves as "Spiritual But Not Religious" (SBNR), 55 percent as "Spiritual," 24.2 percent as "Religious," 3.2 percent as "Humanist," and 3.7 percent as "None of these." Among solitaries, 25.5 percent identified themselves as "Spiritual But Not Religious" (SBNR), 50.4 percent as "Spiritual," 12.4 percent as "Religious," 5.7 percent as "Humanist," and 6 percent as "None of these."

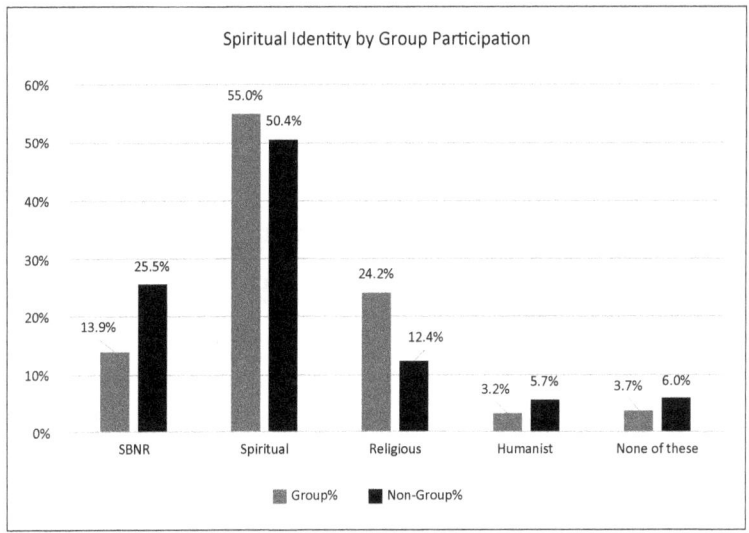

Research Question 4: What are the personal spiritual needs of affiliated and unaffiliated Pagans, respectively?

Only 6.4 percent of respondents said they had no needs with which they might sometimes want spiritual support. "Exploring and deepening personal spirituality" was the most frequently-selected need (73.8 percent). Ceremonial services such as weddings and funerals were indicated by 48.2 percent; support during family, job or health stress, by 46.1 percent; and 37.4 percent indicated a desire for support in learning about their tradition.

Analysis by group affiliation ("Spiritual Needs by Group Participation or Solitary" chart) shows very little difference in perceived spiritual support needs between group and non-group participants. The most noticeable difference may be seen in those who responded, "None." Among group participants, regardless of preference for solitary practice, fewer answered "None."

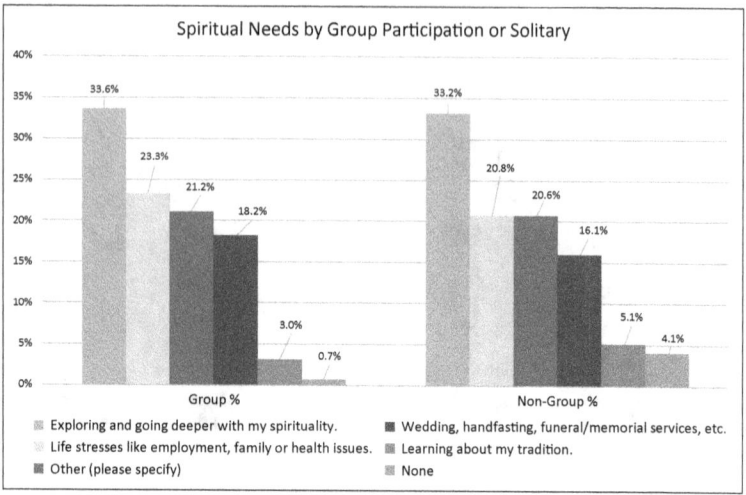

"With what personal needs might you sometimes want spiritual support? (additional comments from all surveys" chart shows categories of added comments ("Other" 9.6 percent) from all surveys. The most frequently mentioned group of comments was the desire for more learning and discussion (14.5 percent), closely followed by a desire for deeper connection to community (13.2 percent). Additional comments indicated perceived needs that ranged from ethical guidance (1.3 percent), to divination and counseling (5.7 percent) to emotional support and friendship (12.6 percent).

Research Question 5: To whom do affiliated and unaffiliated Pagans, respectively, turn for spiritual support?

Group participants ("Spiritual Support Resources By Group Participation or Solitary") showed a preference for turning to a member of their group for spiritual support (33.3 percent), or to the leader of their group (24.7 percent), while 19.5 percent would turn to a friend or family member. Only 1.7 percent would consult a mental health professional, 2.6 percent would turn to someone online, and 3.5 percent selected the answer, "I don't know."

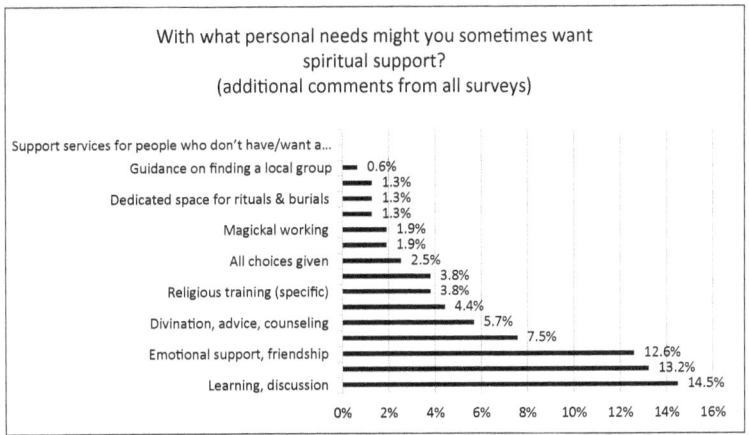

Non-group participants also showed a preference for turning to a friend or family member for spiritual support (41.3 percent). "Someone online" was the choice of 13.5 percent, or something else given in the "Other" comments (15.1 percent). Only 2 percent would turn to their group leader, while 5 percent would turn to another member of the group, and 4.3 percent to a mental health professional. Of these non-group participants, 13.5 percent selected the answer, "I don't know."

Among group participants who indicated that they prefer solitary practice, spiritual support resources were somewhat evenly spread: friend or family member 23.3 percent; group leader 23.3 percent; "Other" (with added comments) 23.3 percent; and another member of the group 20 percent. Those who would turn to a leader in another group were 4.4 percent, 2.2 percent would consult a mental health professional, 1.1

percent would turn to someone online, and 2.2 percent selected the answer, "I don't know."

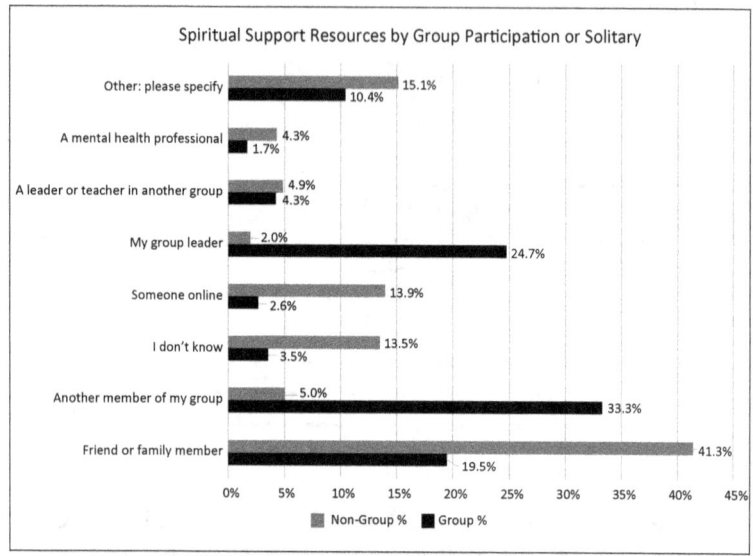

Those who answered that they do not participate in a group and also indicated a preference for solitary practice heavily favored turning to a friend or family member for spiritual support (42.1 percent). Three other choices showed somewhat evenly spread responses: "Other" (with added comments) 16.5 percent; someone online 15.3 percent; and 12.9 percent replied, "I don't know." Only 1.6 percent would turn to their group leader or 4.5 percent to the leader in another group, and 4 percent to a mental health professional. In this data group, only 3.1 percent would turn to another member of their group.

One more set of data, non-group participants who said they were "Unsure" or "Unlikely" to return to a group for any reason, was analyzed by their spiritual support resources. ("Who would you primarily turn to for spiritual support right now? Non-Group who are Unsure or Unlikely to return to a group.")

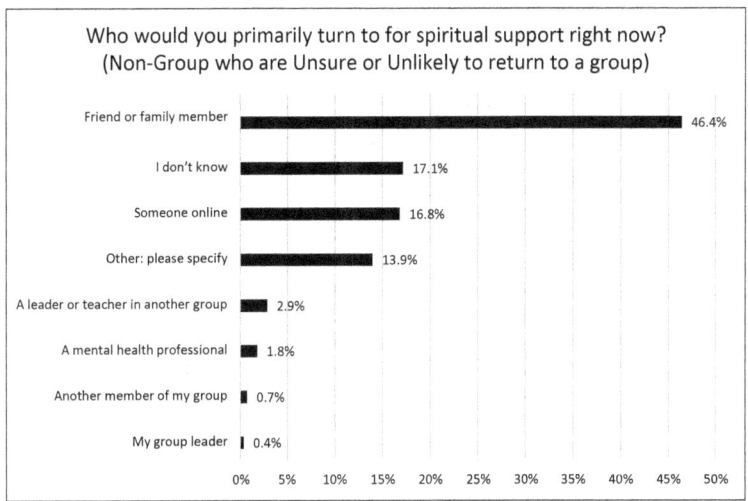

Research Question 6: How might internet activity correlate with spiritual group participation?

As shown in Question 1, 4.3 percent of respondents were part of a group which meets regularly online. However, most survey respondents (74.4 percent) indicated in Question 8 that they connect with others about spirituality online, whether or not they are part of a place-based group. Only 12.6 percent said that they do not do so; another 7 percent said they might connect with others about spirituality if they knew where to go online. Only .4 percent indicated limited internet access. Those who belong to groups outnumber those who do not belong to groups, when it comes to online connection with others about spirituality.

Summary of Results

Participants in the survey identify predominantly as Spiritual or SBNR, or added one of those words to their added description. Most are not part of a local group, though most do participate in some kind of group activity from time to time, such as a festival, workshop or occasional public ritual. Most would prefer to be part of a group, though a significant number choose not to be. Many reasons for avoiding groups could be mitigated through leadership training or more flexible scheduling of group meetings. Some reasons are more intractable, such as social anxiety or fear of sexual harassment. The most common reason for non-participation is the unavailability of a group with which to participate.

Most participants express the desire for accessibility of personal spiritual support, though some appear to have understood the term "spiritual support" to mean accessing guidance internally (through meditation or divination) rather than outside support by a skilled provider such as clergy or a counselor. Developing personal spirituality is the most important support need to participants, perhaps correlating to the high numbers who identify as either Spiritual or SBNR. The desire for at least occasional spiritual support was higher among group participants.

Those who are not part of a group most often turn to a friend or family member for support; those who are part of a group most often turn to another member of that group. Less than one in four group members said they would turn to their own group leader for support.

Virtually all participants have some kind of internet access. While the number of participants who indicated being part of an online group is relatively small, most participants regularly connect online with others about spirituality. Nearly 14 percent of non-group members, and more than 15 percent of non-group members who prefer to be solitary, would turn to an online contact for spiritual support.

Discussion of Results

Group Participation and Preference for Solitary Practice

My original interest was to identify best practices for Pagan ministry. Since Pagan practice is characteristically observed in small groups or by solitary individuals, the researcher sought to obtain updated information about group affiliation and preferences. A wealth of studies by scholars such as Bellah, Roof and Wuthnow, have closely examined religious and community groups, offering both quantitative and qualitative data to guide the development of effective groups. The literature is also seriously considering a constructive response to the rising numbers of Americans who identify as "nones" or "SBNRs," examining the impact of small group programs, non-traditional service times, community program offerings and "lay clergy."

But research which could support recommendations for ministry in Paganism's unique culture was limited, dated or did not exist. Survey data reported here can shed fresh light on the current state of Pagan group participation, non-participation, preference for solitary practice, and the prevalence of participation in virtual groups (online). The collection of extensive qualitative data through comments has yielded a rich resource for better understanding the nuances of Pagan practice in

America. For example, despite the definition of "group" in the survey as something local and place-based, many participants identifying as group members described a cluster of various activities (such as annual festivals, conferences, occult store workshops and online connections) as their group. And some group members say they prefer solitude (without indicating why), yet they are part of a group. Others are solitary, but would prefer to be part of a group.

More than 72 percent of all survey respondents said that they would attend a local group if it were a good fit. But nearly 72 percent of all survey respondents were non-group members, which is close to the 79 percent that Berger found to be solitary in the Pagan Census Revisited.[45] As Berger found with her Census,[46] findings from this new survey show that many non-group participants had been part of a group in the past (21.9 percent), or were part of a group that meets regularly online (4.3 percent).

This leaves unaddressed the needs of Pagans who have no group affiliation. Whether they are solitary by choice or due to some other circumstance, solitaries might represent an overlooked, misunderstood, and/or underserved population. Findings of the survey showed that 58 percent of non-group participants would attend a local group "if it seems like a good fit." This suggests a reconsideration of how best to ensure the sustainability and strength of the overall Pagan

---

[45] James R. Lewis and Inga Tollefsen. "Gender and Paganism in Census and Survey Data," *The Pomegranate: The International Journal of Pagan Studies* 15 (2013) 61–78.

[46] Helen A. Berger, Are Solitaries The Future Of Paganism?" Patheos.com, August 23, 2010. https://www.patheos.com/resources/additional-resources/2010/08/solitaries-the-future-of-paganism.

spiritual community by taking into account the needs of solitaries and possible barriers to participation.

Many comments indicated non-participation or avoidance was related to group dynamics (40.8 percent) or poor leadership (16.2 percent). One comment encompassed the range of concerns expressed about group culture:

> Another reason for ppl [sic] not practicing in groups is that they are poorly socialized. These folks are often asked to leave groups, or the group self-destructs because of this person's influence and the group's (as a whole) inability to deal with problems, either posed by [a] difficult person or other difficulties. Additionally, some groups are led by authoritarian power-trippers who may abuse that position. (Survey participant 6571611511)

Group dynamics and leadership could be improved by education and training of leaders, and by education of all group participants about realistic expectations of leaders and teachers. Appropriate training could also improve issues around sexual harassment, more satisfying ritual and spiritual practice, and accommodation of disabled persons and those with mental health issues.

Impediments to participation which are largely practical, for example, transportation, childcare, meeting time and meeting location, could be addressed through community need surveys, town hall-style Pagan community meetings, better group communication, selective individual communications (e.g., between local leaders) and collaboration among local groups.

Those who indicated issues around increased diversity did not explain whether a respondent was uncomfortable or made to feel unwelcome in a group, or whether the respondent was suggesting that more diverse membership would strengthen the group. In either case, most groups could benefit from diversity training, not unlike that required in many workplaces.

Some respondents expressed concern that Pagan groups should be less church-institutional, or negative past experiences with churches, counselors and others who seemed to impose their religion on the Pagan respondent. This aversion to or even resentment of functioning or being perceived in the same way as a mainstream religious congregation appeared in other comments throughout the survey. Development of best practices in Pagan ministry will need to understand such aversions in order to provide effective recommendations. Keeping in mind the strong feminist, environmentalist, and peace movement influences on Paganism in the 1960s and 1970s,[47] a potential area of further study might be to examine whether concerns about becoming institutional or mainstream are generational, with the possibility that the concerns will diminish over time through generational replacement. Another potential area of study would be to examine what effect routinization and institutionalization might have on Paganism, whether to its detriment or benefit.

One more issue that arose, and which was not anticipated, was the prevalence of individuals who noted "social anxiety" or emotional disorders as a reason for not participating in a group (7.8 percent) or wishing to be solitary (7 percent). It is important for group leaders and Pagan ministers to acknowledge these special needs, and for researchers to take them into consideration when studying ministry best practices.

---

[47] Chas S. Clifton, *Her Hidden Children: The Rise of Wicca and Paganism in America* (Lanham, Md.: AltaMira, 2006).

As in Reece's study,[48] some (14.4 percent) noted the greater commitment required for working with a group. One person positively described their journey through group participation, disaffiliation and more recent group affiliation:

> Basically, they did not have enough flexibility to really work with my true calling...which, no harm, no foul... their primary interest is in perpetuating their particular tradition. I am called by the Gods to do certain things and the work I was doing there was serving more as a distraction and they were not positioned to gain anything from my work. With the groups I am in now, it is mutually beneficial...so it is a good fit. (Survey participant 6531501857)

Even assuming that all who wished to practice with a group were able to do so, there were still a significant number (280) of this non-group data set who were "unsure" they would want to participate in a group (18.9 percent), or "unlikely" to do so (12.4 percent). Among these individuals, only 56 (20 percent) said they had no personal needs with which they might sometimes need spiritual support. Since many such Pagans might find themselves desiring spiritual support in the future, development of ministry best practices should consider how to be available to them without breaching their independent status.

Those serving Pagans may need to reframe their understanding of any population being served. Pagan levels of group participation seem likely to continue the trend of increasing fluidity. While many solitaries in the survey would like to be part of a local group, the difficulties with accessing such participation may

---

48 Gwendolyn Reece, "Prevalence and Importance of Contemporary Pagan Practices," *The Pomegranate: The International Journal of Pagan Studies* 16, no. 1 (201) 12.

contribute to these declining levels of participation. The trend of fluid, self-defined belief and practice suggest that going forward, groups will experience little success with imposed beliefs. Shifting levels of commitment (as well as the high transience of many Americans due to work travel and moves) by Pagans will also challenge groups to adapt. In the future, online community participation may be the only consistent channel for group cohesion.

Online Community

This study found that high numbers of both group and non-group participants take part in some kind of online communication with other Pagans. One respondent directly linked their spiritual growth with online access:

> The online community is growing and available so for information and other points of view, I can go there, often with sources too. Which really is way more helpful than word of mouth, which is often off the cuff and not sourced. I have freedom to not be judged for way of practice, and I can do it at any time, naked clothed whatever. Solitude offers true individuality in spirituality. (Survey participant 6541910887)

Some respondents noted the problems with online trolls (people who post inflammatory remarks for the sake of starting arguments in online groups) or other conflicts. Commenters noted the variation in quality of online contacts, as well as their sometimes superficial nature. Despite these mentioned drawbacks, positive mentions of free access to information and contacts by internet were scattered throughout responses to all survey questions. With its ubiquitous and nearly universal reach in America, use of the internet as an avenue for Pagan ministry and spiritual support should be included in the development of best practices. Examining the decline of coven membership and participation, Ezzy and Berger[49] had proposed the possibility that widespread access to online Pagan activity might be resulting in larger groups but less intense participation and commitment. Since some participants seem to consider their group practice to be some combination of local participation, affiliation with an online group (including social media), visits to festivals and conferences, and occasional attendance at public events, further studies might investigate the rise in internet use compared with the rise in Pagan membership in online groups, as well as with the number of solitaries.

Spiritual Identity

Survey respondents named more than 200 traditions or types of Paganism that they practice. When asked to select one category to describe their spirituality (religious, spiritual, humanist, SBNR, none of these) more than 61 percent added an often-lengthy explanation of their beliefs, and nearly 56 percent wrote in that they identify with their own combination of the choices given, e.g., "I am Humanist and SBNR." Many of the commenters gave a name to their spirituality, such as: Gnostic, Hermetic, Theist, Animist, Mystic, Celtic, and Episco-pagan. The apparent reluctance to conform with even the most general of labels given as choices in this

---

49   Douglas Ezzy and Helen A. Berger, "Witchcraft: Changing Patterns of Participation in the Early Twenty-First Century," *The Pomegranate: The International Journal of Pagan Studies* 11, no. 2 (2009), 165–80.

survey question suggests a growing fluidity of spiritual identity in this country, parallel to that described in the literature about religious participation in general, not just Pagan. Writing in the *Journal of Ecumenical Studies* in 2017,[50] Heim noted that some people are "hybrid in their religious identities and practices," and explore spirituality without necessarily being connected to a religious body. Heim's evaluation would appear to be particularly salient to consideration of Pagan ideas of spiritual identity.

Mercadante[51] found that SBNRs usually insist that spirituality is personal and religion is institutional, even though that is not an academic distinction. Survey comments take this idea even further, indicating a perception that the word "religion" signals control, manipulation, dogma, insincerity, and even abuse. The implication is that "spiritual" somehow avoids these traps, as if they are unique to established or institutionalized religions. Here is a typical comment on this theme:

> I respect and value the rituals, community, and self-improvement aspects of most religions, but thoroughly reject a hierarchical approach to spirituality due to numerous bad experiences with toxic spiritual leaders from both pagan and Christian traditions. (Survey participant 6542647568)

Wuthnow[52] noted that individualism carries with it a burden of responsibility to balance self-interest and

---

50 S. M. Heim, "Of Two Minds about a Theology without Walls." *Journal of Ecumenical Studies* 51, no. 4 (2017), 479–86.

51 Linda Mercadante, *Belief without Borders: Inside the Minds of the Spiritual but not Religious* (Oxford: Oxford University Press, 2014).

52 Robert Wuthnow, *Loose Connections: Joining Together in America's Fragmented Communities* (Cambridge, Mass.: Harvard University Press, 2002).

commitment. Many of the survey participants made clear that they do not perceive or anticipate a benefit from group commitment. The previous section quotes a survey participant who wrote, "Solitude offers true individuality in spirituality" (Survey participant 6541910887). But the mistrust that has emerged from such attitudes (some understandably derived from damaging group experience) may not only be preventing some individuals from enjoying a positive group affiliation, but may also have damaged social ties, lessened civility and removed the social barriers to dysfunctional behavior provided by religious and spiritual groups.

Development of Pagan ministry best practices must examine these dynamics if effective strategies are to be developed. As in mainstream Christian and Jewish organizations, leaders must balance their ideals of how group participation should look with the reality of the actual needs and desires of potential group members. Assuming that static Pagan group models are likely to prove as ineffectual in the future as unchanging congregational models have been for Christians and Jews. Building flexibility into ministry methods will be a necessary challenge in order for Pagan groups to remain relevant and resilient.

Spiritual fluidity of identity may be the strongest factor in how Pagans perceive group affiliation. It may also account for why fewer in the survey identify as strictly solitary because, while in the years since Berger's and Reece's studies affiliation with groups across all religions in America has decreased sharply, most Americans still assert that they have religious or spiritual beliefs.

Findings appear to affirm that American Pagan practice resembles what Coco called "networked individualism," internet connections serving to transform relationships, which were formerly only found in local groups, into more broadly-based communities of practice. These findings might, indeed, bear up Ezzy and Berger's suggestion that internet-based community can be much larger but, as they theorize, they may also represent less intense commitment and participation, further eroding the benefit groups might provide.

The lack of hesitation by survey respondents to personally redefine the meanings of group affiliation and solitary practice signals a sea change in how to identify best practices for Pagan ministry. While Pagan culture is distinct and often oppositional to mainstream culture, it is still likely that many Pagans share the desire for belonging to a community of spiritually like-minded people which was voiced by a significant portion of respondents to the General Social Survey of 2016. Researchers will need to understand the complexities of multiple religious identities, multiple ways of perceiving affiliation, wide variation in commitment and participation expectations, and a range of what members might expect from groups and their leaders.

A troubling result from the survey was the concern raised about racism in groups, as well as those who either said their group mission was to build racially-identified groups or who listed such a group as their religious affiliation. It may be tempting to view this data as anomalous or statistically-insignificant. However, as I worked on this study the infamous Charlottesville March and murder took place, many more unarmed blacks have been shot by police, a fraternity was suspended from Syracuse University due to racist videos, and tee-shirts celebrating Dylann Roof (the Mother Emanuel Charleston shooter) were removed from online sale. There is a startling rise of Pagan symbols and cooption of Pagan theology among racist groups both in America and in Europe.[53] It may be prudent, therefore, to view survey data as a harbinger, and respond by developing strategies to thwart racism in Pagan groups, and by educating Pagan leaders to implement such strategies.

The Pew Research Center's Religion & Public Life Project[54] estimates 34 percent of all Americans identify themselves now as SBNR. This survey cannot assume a correlation between American SBNRs and American Pagan solitaries, who appear to be far more numerous at this time. Nevertheless, the parallel occurrence in both groups calls for further attention. These dramatic changes in overall religious identity are likely to prompt research and strategies for ministering to SBNRs which could prove useful to Pagans as they develop their own strategies for spiritually supporting solitary or loosely-affiliated Pagans.

Spiritual Support Needs and Resources

"Exploring and going deeper with my spirituality" was the most common choice of reasons for seeking spiritual support (74.8 percent). This result underscores the strong value placed on learning by Pagans, as shown in Berger's Pagan Census Revisited finding that Pagans are generally well-educated.[55] Comparison

---

53 Michael Strmiska, personal communication, February 16, 2018.
54 Cary Funk and Greg Smith, "'Nones' on the Rise," Pew Forum on Religion & Public Life. 2012.
55 James R. Lewis and Inga Tollefsen. "Gender and Paganism, " 61–78.

of the spiritual support needs across group and non-group participants showed very close results. Both groups would seem to desire generally the same kinds of spiritual support.

> Some expressed strong negative opinions about consulting a trained counselor or therapist, or even another person. Many answered similarly to this commenter, "Myself, and that's all I need." Another seemed to suggest that spiritual support was only needed if one was religious, "Not applicable. I am an atheist now so I have no need for spiritual support." (Survey participant 6554134953)

A friend or family member is the most common resource that survey respondents turn to for spiritual support. Far more non-group participants and those who prefer solitary practice would turn to a friend or family member than those who are group participants. Survey choices and comments most commonly suggest a desire for support from someone not part of the respondent's spiritual group or geographic community, but who understands Pagan religion and culture.

Asked what was helpful during past experiences with spiritual support, participants emphasized listening and emotional support, which are the most important tools of a trained counselor or chaplain. Unhelpful experiences noted unskilled providers, rigid attitudes of a provider, and the imposition of the providers' personal beliefs. An area for further research might be to determine whether the majority of respondents are aware of the choices of spiritual support which might be available, what might be expected in such an encounter, and the difference between friend and community support, and support by someone with appropriate training. Pagan leaders should also be trained in active listening, as well as understanding when and how to refer someone to an appropriate professional or other resource.

Implications for Practice

Most Pagans express a desire to be part of a Pagan group, but vary in their perceptions and definitions of group participation and affiliation. Barriers to group practice include factors which can be addressed (e.g., with training), some which are practical (e.g., transportation, disability), and some which may require special support to accommodate (e.g., social anxiety). There is a need for development of ministry standards which would make respectful spiritual support available to those who have a specific preference for solitary practice. Effective ministry and spiritual support of Pagans should probably involve a combination of online contact, local activities, and occasional special events like public rituals, conferences, and social events.

Any approach to Pagan ministry in the near future must take into account the following factors:

- The strong value of individualism by many Pagans;
- The strong mistrust of authority by many Pagans;
- The still-nascent and -evolving definitions of Pagan religions and spiritualities, including a tendency to self-define oppositionally (as what one is not); and
- The lack of broadly-accepted standards and training for Pagan leaders.

Researchers of religious trends have shown clearly that Americans' religious participation has both decreased and dramatically changed from congregational membership to individual personal spirituality. This study has shown the likelihood of a similar tendency among American Pagans, most of whom now refer to themselves as "solitary," some by choice, and some out of necessity. As society has changed from localized affiliations to highly-fluid affinity-based associations, many of them distant or virtual (online), most religious groups and services have done little to adjust, including Pagan groups.

During the last century, a time when many of our current expectations about religious affiliation and ministry congealed, most Americans were still close to, or only steps removed from, rural-agricultural life and small-town life. They tended to stay in jobs for a lifetime (or aspired to do so), stay in the same marriage, and affiliate with, volunteer for, and make charitable gifts to local organizations, including religious congregations. Ministry methods have, therefore, been developed around the existence of local affiliations and relationship ties. Even witchcraft covens of the last century relied on geographic proximity, group meetings, and individual interactions among members. Only since the 1990s has the widespread availability of online access altered this pattern.

Coco's work articulates a compelling vision of the Pagan community as "a web of interactive nodes in online and offline places".[56] Her vision neither disparages the loss of former affiliative patterns, nor promotes new ones, but provides for at least one religion the valuable new map of religious terrain called for by

---

56 Angela Coco, "Pagan Religiousness as 'Networked Individualism,'" in *Spirituality: Theory, Praxis and Pedagogy*, ed. Robert Fisher and Daniel Riha (Leiden: Brill, 2012), 125–36.

scholars such as Roof.[57] Since societal change appears destined to continue at the past century's rate of acceleration, there is reason to assume that networked individualism may in the future no longer serve as a good description of Pagan community. But while it does, we need to adapt. The Christian Bible cautions against putting new wine into old wineskins because the new wine could bubble and burst an old skin. Likewise, it is unrealistic to expect that the habits of a former time will serve us in the same way in such a changed society. The things that remain unchanged are the human spirit, the search for meaning, the need for compassion, and the desire to serve; these deserve more flexible, responsive frameworks for support.

Using Coco's ideas as a springboard, I propose a new theory of "constellated ministry," which acknowledges the dramatic changes in American Pagan affiliations. Affiliations are now largely driven by the individual, rather than by the organization or group. As an example, a picture of one Pagan's network might include this hypothetical constellation of affinities: training and initiations in two different traditions; a desire to engage in both corporate and solitary religious practices; health needs which discourage or prohibit long walks to an isolated ritual location; a love of group singing; enjoyment and habit of lifelong learning; interest in ancient history; amateur birdwatching and naturalist activities; passion for LGBTQ rights; concern for urban revitalization; and interest in local voluntarism. These interests and needs represent the points of entry,

---

57 Wade Clark Roof, *Spiritual Marketplace: Baby Boomers and the Remaking of American Religion* (Princeton: Princeton University Press, 2001).

or interactive nodes, for engagement with this sample individual.

Some nodes may overlap: perhaps, birdwatching and group singing with a local senior center by an ad hoc group of local Pagans from various traditions. That same group may join with other groups for occasional joint rituals and workshops, or offer themselves as choral backup for a special community ritual. The individual may pursue learning about Minoan culture through an online course where she meets people from various states, Canada, Belgium, Lebanon, and Italy, in the process discovering a Lebanese person interested in pre-Canaanite religions who wishes to stay in touch and share ritual ideas. As someone interested in bettering her society, this person has many online connections to social justice advocates in her community. When there is an important rally, calls to be made to elected officials, or a need for workers at an emergency shelter, she turns to her online Pagan network with a call for action, or simply to share information. She may hold a Pagan learning group in her home for a year, to explore leadership issues with local Pagan leaders. Note that each of these nodes is a point of bidirectional interaction, that is, some interaction is initiated by the individual, and other interactions originate externally.

Where in this map does ministry occur? Paganism has no tradition of trained professional ministers, but this study reveals the shortcomings of untrained leaders and resulting erosion of community which could otherwise provide spiritual support. Pagans who decide to serve as chaplains and pursue a traditional seminary education are seldom perceived as a resource to the Pagan community, even if the community is aware of their work with a hospital, the armed forces, or a hospice. If, as this study showed, most Pagans are solitary and most have personal needs with which they may desire spiritual support, the network nodes must serve as new channels for giving and receiving that support. Ministry must consist of a constellation of nodes by which trained leadership and those who desire support may access each other, both actively and passively.

The study shows that group affiliation is still important to many Pagans, even if they are unable to be part of a group. This suggests that local group gatherings will continue to be an important part of Pagan spiritual life, so both leaders and groups, respectively, should actively pursue the education and training recommendations given below. Pastoral education usually teaches leaders appropriate and effective ways to work with the disabled, parents and children, the mentally ill, and other special populations, or refer them to professional resources. Yet such training is not usually accessed by Pagans even though these populations are found throughout the Pagan community. Pagan leaders, in particular, should actively seek education by qualified professionals, to better provide support to individuals and guidance to Pagan groups. Research using pre- and post-testing of groups implementing the recommendations of this study could support the development of proven-effective practices and mitigate concerns shared by participants in this study.

Although the efficacy of online groups is still being debated, this study showed that many Pagans participate in such groups, and for some, that is their only option for live group participation. Some Pagan leaders have already employed this method of outreach for several years; a constellated ministry should consider making such a group or groups available.

Those who wish to offer spiritual support or ministry to Pagans should develop communication channels by which they may be easily accessed. Such channels must respect the autonomy and privacy of Pagans or others who choose to contact a Pagan minister or leader for assistance. With less than half a percent of Pagans lacking internet access, online and phone communications will be an important component of communication channels. Websites, social media pages, and online listings, will facilitate passive ministry, allowing leaders to respond to those who request support. Web content pushed by feeds, podcasts, Youtube channels, online courses, and webinar presentations and meetings can facilitate active ministry initiated by a Pagan leader.

An additional way to actively provide support to the Pagan community is to develop widely-available curricula for study which clarifies traditions, teaches the skills noted in education and training recommendations below, and provides extended education about related topics, e.g., history of a region and culture from which a tradition is based, or reading and discussion of world sacred texts. Such curricula could provide guidance and structure for CUUPS groups, ADF groves and protogroves, independent circles and covens, prison Pagan groups, and more.

A last recommendation is the importance of leaders and groups engaging in deliberate cultivation of community ties, both intrafaith (within Pagan communities) and interfaith (relationships with leaders and members of other religions), as well as various local and regional organizations which may be good allies or project partners (e.g., a food bank or the riverkeeper). Local community ties can prove to be valuable resources during a crisis, or when local Pagan individuals and groups do not have sufficient critical mass to be effective in a cause. Partnerships with non-Pagans can go a long way towards alleviating fears that still prevent many Pagans from participating in open events, or revealing their religion to a hospital chaplain. Partnerships with both Pagan and non-Pagan community groups can improve and enrich mutual understanding between groups which previously misunderstood each other.

Education and Training Recommendations

The study is intended to be a resource for developing and testing best practices in ministry to Pagans. Recommended areas of training include:

a) Education and training specifically for leaders (see topics below);
b) Ways to better understand and accommodate those with disabilities;
c) Ways to better understand and accommodate those mental illness;
d) How to be available to solitaries desiring spiritual support, and how to do so without breaching their independent status;
e) Development of programming recommendations which facilitate a complementary mix of activities, a constellated ministry, that supports networked individualism;
f) Development of online networks which connect disparate groups with each other and with solitaries, facilitating intergroup communication, cooperation and collaboration.

Recommendations for educating and training leaders:

a) Active-supportive listening and other traditional chaplaincy skills;
b) Leadership, ethics, clergy standards, and group dynamics;
c) How to develop community networks and communicate effectively;
d) Cultural diversity and sensitivity, including avoidance of sexually-inappropriate behavior;
e) Basics of mental health awareness, how to identify potential issues and refer out;
f) How to develop flexible programming; and when developed.

Best Practices for Pagan Ministry

The wider Pagan community will benefit from information and trainings to enhance awareness of:

a) Realistic and appropriate expectations of group leaders, including understanding the difference between spiritual support, Pagan priesthood, and other Pagan leadership;
b) Appropriate expectations of spiritual support from group leaders, professionals, and family or friends;
d) Cultural diversity and sensitivity, including avoidance of sexually-inappropriate behavior, and sensitivity to those with disabilities, and those with mental illness;
e) Non-professional spiritual leadership training for those serving local communities.

Organizational Recommendations

a) Colleges, seminaries, community organizations and any others who provide training and education in the topics noted above should use this study to guide development of curricula, and to adapt as needed for the unique Pagan culture;
b) Seminaries should lead a broad-based task force for developing a set of standards for Pagan ministry;
c) Seminaries (both traditional and Pagan) should look at ways to adapt their current programs to address changing Pagan practice and needs;
d) Pagan organizations should create resources for offering the training noted above and, where needed, identify partners who can provide appropriate training;
e) Consider partnering with local, regional and/or national social justice organizations to develop Pagan community efforts to address sexual harassment and racism in Pagan groups.

Conclusion

The study has raised questions that may be examined with future research:

- What effect do routinization and institutionalization have on Paganism (past, present and future), both detrimental and beneficial?
- How does the rise in internet use compare with the rise in Pagan membership in online groups, and with the number of solitary practitioners? Is there a causal effect? Is such a potential effect positive, neutral or detrimental?

- How do Pagans use multiple religious identities to form new theologies?
- What can be learned from survey participants who indicated a desire for support while "exploring and deepening" their spirituality?
- Further development of the theory of constellated ministry.

I will close with the reminder that most Americans still consider themselves either religious, spiritual, or feeling that there is a meaning beyond physical existence despite their lack of religious identity or affiliation. At some point in their lives, even "nones" are likely to feel the need for spiritual support. Pagans are still defining themselves and their religion, but share the human tendency to look for support as they search for meaning, and during life traumas. The unique nature of Pagan culture calls for specialized ways of ministry adapted to Pagan needs and concerns. It is hoped that in the near future, recommendations from the study will be widely implemented, building the resiliency and effectiveness of existing Pagan groups, providing better support for Pagan group participants as well as Pagan solitaries, and strengthening the overall fabric of our communal religious-spiritual life in America.

Index

abuse, domestic 95, 96–98
abuse, sexual 25, 95, 96–98
abuse, signs of 98
abuse, substance *see addiction*
accessibility *see disabilities*
accountability 58, 94–95
addiction 99–101
allies and partners 47, 112–114, 168
allies, sources of and how to develop 76–77
authority, religious or clerical 14

best practices in Pagan ministry 129, 151, 159, 163

change, preparing for and adapting 61–62, 66–67, 84, 114, 164–165
chaplaincy, as a ministry model 19, 38
chaplaincy, types of 18–19
clergy, burnout 55, 57–58
clergy, Pagan ambivalence towards 34–35
clergy, Pagan roles and expectations 23, 32, 33, 68–70, 106–107, 135–138, 145–148
communications, to engage participation 43, 46, 59, 82, 168
communications, to preserve tradition and lore 60

communities of practice, Pagan groups and 40
community, festivals and conferences as 28
community, online 17–18, 41, 43, 63, 77–79, 131, 149, 151, 156–157, 164
community, place-based 29
confidentiality and privacy 47, 78
conflict, in Pagan communities 24, 57
consent culture 95–96
constellated ministry, leadership constellation 46, 112
constellated ministry, network nodes 43, 59, 79–83, 164, 164
constellated ministry, theory of 44–48, 118–119, 165–167
coronavirus (COVID 19) 115–116
counseling, pastoral 105–107
counseling, regulation 106
countercultural attitude 24
credentials 106–107
culture differences, respect 92–94

disabilities, accommodation of 91–92
disabilities, laws regarding 91
disaster, spiritual care in 18, 102, 119

domestic violence *see abuse, domestic*
drugs *see abuse, substance*

education and training needed by Pagan leaders 29, 58, 66, 108-111, 153, 167, 169-170
engagement platforms, 40, 48, 59, 60 *see also constellated ministry, network nodes*

globalization 36-37
gravitational theory 39-41
groups, benefits of affiliation 4, 9-10, 61, 65-66, 88
groups, barriers to participation 25, 62, 142, 143, 153
groups, dysfunction and poor leadership in 24, 56, 86, 89-90
groups, Pagan definition of 152, 157, 160
groups, small group movement 3, 14-16
groups, vulnerabilities 62

identity, religious multiple and fluid 12-13, 159-160
individualism, networked 43, 160
individualism and autonomy, Pagan 24, 26, 163
individualism, tension between community and autonomy 4, 27, 158-159
individualism, U.S. culture of 27
infrastructure 14, 16, 42
interfaith, 6-7, 47, 62

leadership, cultivating in others 48, 51, 60
leadership, Pagan 49-54

mental health 4, 19, 42, 75, 98, 110, 153-154, 170
military, Pagans 18
military trauma *see moral injury*
ministry, and adaptability 66, 159, 164-165
ministry, best practices Pagan 6, 7, 104-105
ministry, contested term 7-8, 33, 118
ministry, dual roles 35
ministry, meaning for Pagans 41-43, 45, 63-64
moral injury 101-102

Pagan, contested term 21
Pagans, bias against 26, 29, 30
Pagans, characteristics 21, 29-30, 138-140
Pagans, concealment, privacy and secrecy 25, 29, 46, 47, 59, 67, 168
Pagans, group or solitary 43, 85, 131-134, 141-142, 152
Pagans, individualism 29
Pagans, mistrust of authority 24, 26, 29, 159, 163
Pagans, prevalence 20
Pagans, self-definition 22, 130, 157-158, 160, 163
Pagans, sexuality 31
Pagans, spiritual support needs and preferences 32, 85, 106, 135-138, 145-148, 161-163
Paganism, contemporary development of 2, 154, 163
Paganism, racism found in 142, 160-161
Paganism, traditions of 22, 139, 157-158
pandemic *see coronavirus*

Index

partners *see allies and partners*
planning, *see strategic planning*
Post traumatic stress disorder (PTSD) 101

Regulation *see counselling, regulation*
religion, commercialization of 26
religion, decline in affiliation across religions 41, 163
religion, hierarchy and control 22–23
resources 78–79, 111, 120

sacred texts, lack of Pagan 23
sexual harassment 25, 109, 142, 143, 150, 153 *see also abuse, sexual*
social media 17, 46, 78, 82, 168
social trust 10, 16
spiritual but not religious (SBNR), and Pagans 3, 6, 12, 144, 161
spirituality, contrast with religion 11, 22, 158

spiritual support needs of Pagans *see Pagans, spiritual needs*
starting your ministry 71–77
strategic planning, appreciative inquiry 84
strategic planning, environmental scan 74–79
strategic planning, personal discernment process 71–74
strategic planning, self-reflection 71–74
spirituality, multiple and blended 12–13, 21, 29, 138, 160

technology, effect on religious life 16–18, 46, 59, 63, 88, 149, 156–157, 167–168
training *see education and training*
trauma, crime victims 102–104
trauma, intergenerational 97–8
trolls and antagonists 90–91, 156

victims of crime *see trauma, crime victims*

www.ingramcontent.com/pod-product-compliance
Lightning Source LLC
Chambersburg PA
CBHW071847230426
43671CB00012B/2092